FORMULA 1

DRIVE TO SURVIVE

THE UNOFFICIAL COMPANION

FORMULA 1

DRIVE TO SURVIVE

THE UNOFFICIAL COMPANION

THE STARS,
STRATEGY,
TECHNOLOGY,
AND HISTORY OF F1

Stuart Codling

CONTENTS

Chapter 1

THE HUMAN TOUCH
THE PEOPLE BEHIND F1

Formula 1 is a people business as well as a technical one. Some teams employ over 1,000 staff, of which just seventy to eighty form the traveling contingent who operate the cars. While the twenty drivers form the principal cast of TV broadcasts and are the focus of fan attention, this is a team sport in which an organization is only as strong as its weakest link.

Wider TV coverage and the growth of specialist media, as well as the greater reach of the social media age, have created new stars—faces that are often seen, but whose reasons for being there are perhaps not so widely understood. What do these people do? And how do they fit into the twenty-first-century version of a racing endeavor whose teams used to consist of few enough people to fit into a reasonably sized family car?

Christian Horner, team principal Red Bull Racing; Toto Wolff, team principal and CEO Mercedes AMG F1 GP; Mattia Binotto, team principal of Scuderia Ferrari, at the Grand Prix of Monaco from May 23 to 26, 2019, in Monaco. Although there is a certain respect among them all, the competitiveness between them is staggering.

Team Principal

If *Drive to Survive* can be considered a soap opera, the team principals fulfill the role of authority figure—usually in conflict or otherwise having to conduct some sort of firefighting operation. *DTS* gleefully amplifies some of the friction between these characters. At times during season 1, it feels as though Red Bull's Christian Horner and Renault's Cyril Abiteboul are about to reenact the scene from *Dynasty* in which Krystal and Alexis Carrington came to blows in a lily pond.

There are distinct parallels between the obsessive rancor Horner holds for Mercedes team principal Toto Wolff in latter episodes and the Bobby Axelrod/Chuck Rhoades dynamic in *Billions*. Appropriate, indeed, for a job which touches every aspect of a F1 team's operations, including the vital issue of the millions of dollars that must be earned and spent. While corporate structures vary—some teams have CEOs to whom the team principals report—this is a day-to-day leadership role. The team principal carries ultimate responsibility for the success of trackside operations and the quality of the car that comes from the factory—and the identity of who will drive it.

Cyril Abiteboul, Renault Sport F1 managing director and Christian Horner, team principal of Red Bull Racing, on the grid during the during the Bahrain Grand Prix, 2018. The Red Bull/Renault relationship was already teetering as Horner would switch the team to Honda engines the following year.

Formula 1 Drive to Survive: The Unofficial Companion

It is famously said that "It Takes a Village." And to play in F1, it takes more like a nation. This is just an example of the team members that are brought to work at the track; behind the scenes with the team's XQ, engine provider, and additional swarms of engineers to design and build a car, and make it into a race, much less win.

Claire Williams, daughter of Sir Frank Williams, Williams F1 team founder and principal, took over the primary leadership role of the team in 2012. Until its sale in 2020, Williams was the last family-owned team in Formula 1.

Mercedes AMG F1 Team Principal Toto Wolff having a word (or three) with his multi-championship-winning star racehorse Lewis Hamilton at the 2018 Grand Prix of Russia, a race that the latter went on to win on the path to his fifth F1 world title.

Gone are the days when the team principal's name was above the door as owner rather than employee. But the stakes are just as high, the commitment and chemistry similarly important. Take, for example, McLaren's journey in the seasons covered by the *Drive to Survive* cameras.

McLaren had dispensed with the traditional team principal role in favor of a race director reporting to a CEO who, in turn, reported to McLaren Group chairman and CEO Ron Dennis—himself formerly the team principal. There were too many leaders. By the time the *DTS* cameras were rolling, Dennis had been ousted in a boardroom coup and tension simmered throughout the organization. In "Trouble at the Top" (S1:E5), Dennis's replacement, American entrepreneur Zak Brown, is seen struggling to get a grip on the chaos—and sporting director Eric Boullier ultimately takes the fall.

The Daily Mail, a British newspaper, was a keen agitator against Boullier and was the source of the scoop that became known as "Freddo-gate," when disgruntled McLaren employees revealed that inexpensive chocolates were part of an informal incentive scheme presided over by an out-of-touch management. *Mail* journalist Jonathan McEvoy is the unnamed voice in the press conference featured in the episode, pressing Boullier on whether he ought to quit.

Another restructuring followed in which Brown headhunted the well-regarded Andreas Seidl from Porsche to act as team principal in a more conventional management system with "straight lines" of reporting, as Seidl put it. He quickly won back the dressing room: You can see how he leads from the front in later seasons, such as staying on in Melbourne to ensure the safe return of his stricken crew when the pandemic hits at the beginning of season 3, to revving up the entire squad when they pose for a team photo in the wake of Daniel Ricciardo's victory at Monza in season 4.

Frenchman Eric Boullier, McLaren F1's racing director, paid the price for the team's struggles in 2017.

American Zak Brown, McLaren executive
director, left, and Andreas Seidl, McLaren
team principal, on the grid at the 2022
Spanish Grand Prix have made great strides
in retooling McLaren F1 to its long
standing as a team that could, on any
given day, bring home a race win. McLaren
returned to the use of Mercedes engine
power, and its driver lineup balances hot
young talent with proven race winners.

" THE WERE TOO MANY
LEADERS."

Team Manager

While the team principal wields executive power, the team manager—sometimes called the sporting director—has a less public-facing, but no less critical, role in the day-to-day running of the organization. Between races they're responsible for all the logistics of getting the cars, their components, all the team gear, and the team itself around the world to the various races—a job that's now even more of a tangle as the number of events grows and more inventory needs to go by sea freight for environmental reasons. Paperwork is also the curse of the team manager, whether that's ensuring team equipment can cross borders without being confiscated or hit with import-export duties, or even applying for drivers' "superlicenses."

Trackside, the team manager is responsible for the operational well-being of the organization. Fractures can develop between individuals when they're away from home, traveling, and working together under pressure.

The team manager also has to carry the sport's regulations around in their head. F1's procedural rules can be arcane and the team manager needs to ensure his organization is compliant at all times—and sometimes remind the stewards and race director what the rules are. Through the 2021 season, more radio traffic between the teams and the FIA was broadcast, bringing the voices of these generally unsung individuals to the fore. Indeed, Red Bull sporting director Jonathan Wheatley became pivotal in the soap opera of the championship run-in, aggressively lobbying the race director in Saudi Arabia and Abu Dhabi.

There's very little churn of team managers; the majority have been in racing for years and worked their way up. Wheatley and his counterpart at Mercedes, Ron Meadows, are typical in that they began their motorsport lives as mechanics. Wheatley was chief mechanic at what is now Alpine before he became team manager at Red Bull in 2006; Meadows has been at Mercedes since their previous incarnation as British American Racing and had a role in building and kitting out the factory.

"Which of us is going to win today" might be the topic of conversation among Mercedes GP Team Manager Ron Meadows (left) and Jonathan Wheatley, Red Bull Racing sporting director, at the 2022 British Grand Prix. It turns out neither got to drink the champagne that day as Carlos Sainz Jr. drove his Ferrari home to a team win and his first F1 victory.

Among the most successful of all
modern-times Team Supremos is Jean Todt,
seen here with wife, actress Michelle
Yeoh. He orchestrated Michael Schumacher's
championship years with Ferrari and spent
over a decade as FIA president.

Technical Director

In the very distant past, a single person could design pretty much every aspect of an F1 car. Top-level motor racing is now so sophisticated, high-tech, and intricately detailed that no individual could possibly have the time to draw every component. Nevertheless the buck has to stop somewhere and that's why the technical director earns the big bucks.

This role blends engineering vision with hands-on people management. The technical director sets the engineering philosophy and is responsible for ensuring their (often vast) team of designers and aerodynamicists deliver on all the performance and weight targets.

Most technical directors come from an aerodynamics background and several have been pivotal in major advances over the past three decades. Mercedes's Mike Elliott, for example, was the team's head of aerodynamics until he stepped up when his predecessor, James Allison, moved to the chief technical officer role. Allison himself is a former aero man, and at Ferrari he pioneered the vital but unsung role of trackside aerodynamicist, now a vital link in the chain between track and factory, ratifying whether simulation work is reflected in real-life lap times.

Perhaps the most famous F1 engineering guru is Red Bull's Adrian Newey, whose background includes stints as both an aerodynamicist and a race engineer. This has given him an unparalleled vision for a car's complete performance. It's a measure of how valuable he is to the team that whenever he undergoes one of his periodic phases of being disenchanted with F1 (he hates tight rules that stifle creativity), Red Bull allows him to step away and do something else, whether that is getting involved with America's Cup yachts or collaborating with Aston Martin on the design of the Valkyrie road car.

Adrian Newey (left) is among the greatest ever Grand Prix race car designers, thus more than qualified to serve as Red Bull Racing's chief technical officer.

F1 Figures

Gordon Murray

The superstar designer of the 1970s and 1980s, South African engineer Gordon Murray was a true maverick: instinctive, creative, and capable of prodigious quantities of work. His innovations weren't always successful (his attempt to get rid of radiators in favor of surface-mounted heat exchangers on the 1978 Brabham BT46 didn't work out), but his work was widely copied. He's rightly famous for the controversial "fan car," which generated downforce through suction, and for the beautiful championship-winning Brabham BT52—which he designed from scratch, almost singlehandedly, in six weeks when a last-minute rule change scuppered his plans for the season. Murray also had a hand in the McLaren MP4/4, which won fifteen of sixteen races in 1988.

Car designer and technical director extraordinaire Gordon Murray debriefs with Argentine ace Carlos Reutemann aboard his Brabham F1 machine at the Germany Grand Prix of 1973.

Head of Engineering

Red Bull Racing's Chief Engineer, Car Engineering, Jonathan Wheatley turns away from his many video monitors and computer screens to follow the pit action behind him at the 2022 Grand Prix dell'Emelia-Romagna at Imola. It turned out to be a great day for Red Bull, with team drivers Verstappen and Perez finishing 1–2.

When *Drive to Survive* takes you into the inner sanctum of a team's trackside operations, either in the formal postsession debriefs or casual backstage chats, among the calmer voices you'll hear will be those of the heads of engineering. When misfortune strikes on the track and the camera cuts to the inevitable shot of the team principal with their head in their hands, the head of engineering will be one of the figures in the background with their eyes still focused on the monitors. This job requires focus, mental discipline, and often a PhD.

Sitting below the technical director, the head of engineering is responsible for managing all the disparate on-site engineering activities—aerodynamics, tires, chassis, electronics—to maximize the car's performance. Back at the factory they project-manage development, managing the different departments such as vehicle science and vehicle performance. Some larger teams split the trackside and factory-based functions between two people.

Since this role blends hard-edged academia with soft skills such as people management, its practitioners tend to stay in place for a long time. Mercedes's performance director, Mark Ellis, spent six years at the team in their previous incarnation at BAR-Honda and then returned in 2014 after a six-year stint at Red Bull; the team's head of trackside engineering, Andrew Shovlin, joined BAR in 1999 and race-engineered Jenson Button. Aston Martin's Tom McCullough joined the team under their previous owner in 2014 as head of trackside engineering, a role that has now become performance director as the team expands through fresh investment.

As a smaller team, Haas expect head of engineering Ayao Komatsu to cover both trackside and factory roles. He is a regular sight on *DTS* by virtue of his proximity to combustible team principal Guenther Steiner.

Just prior to the beginning of a race, the person a driver may spend the most time talking with is his race engineer. Here Haas F1 Team Race Engineer Ayao Komatsu (left) confers with team driver Kevin Magnussen just prior to the start of the 2019 Russian Grand Prix; at times both "Mags" and the Haas machine have shown promise with a handful of credible finishes, yet much work remains to achieve the podium finishes and race wins they both desire.

" THE CALMER VOICES YOU'LL HEAR WILL BE THOSE OF THE HEADS OF ENGINEERING. "

Race Engineer

An integral part of each driver's support system is their race engineer, who acts as the conduit between the driver and the team's operational staff. Like the physiotherapist (or physio, see page 24), the race engineer has an intensely personal relationship with the driver. It's another job that intertwines technical expertise with soft skills: a key role of the job is to communicate with the driver, understand what they're saying about the behavior of the car, and then find practical means of adjusting the car to improve it.

During races the engineer will generally be the driver's sole point of communication with the team, since it's considered best practice not to have many voices competing for the driver's ear while they're at work. Viewers will therefore be familiar with some key voices, if not their faces: the likes of Peter Bonnington (Lewis Hamilton) and Giampero Lambiase (Max Verstappen), for example.

There are exceptions to these rules. Often the team principal will radio the driver after the checkered flag to congratulate or commiserate. At Mercedes, sometimes chief strategist James Vowles will speak, generally to apologize to Hamilton if there's been a strategic blunder (the team knows the best way to handle Lewis is to let him blow off some steam and move on), or to emphasize to the other driver the gravity of a team order ("Valtteri, it's James" has become a social media meme, referring to Hamilton's sometimes recalcitrant former teammate Valtteri Bottas). During the 2020 season Bottas requested more vocal support from Merc team principal Toto Wolff, which is why Wolff stepped up his on-track communications.

And here's another area where the engineer's role overlaps with that of the physio: driver psychology. They're dealing with gifted individuals in high-stress situations, which is why the tone of their radio messages sounds much like that of an airline pilot addressing their passengers. If a driver is struggling to extract the maximum from the car, changing their race engineer is one lever the team management can pull. It goes unmentioned in "Growing Pains" (S4: E7), where Alpine driver Esteban Ocon's performance comes under scrutiny, but one of the changes that contributed to his turnaround in 2021 was the arrival of new race and performance engineers Josh Peckett and Stuart Barlow. His previous engineer, Mark Slade, had worked with world champions Mika Häkkinen and Kimi Räikkönen in the past, but it appeared this relationship with Ocon didn't gel in the same way.

F1 racers are often avid cyclists. They're naturally predispositioned toward anything with wheels that can go fast and to be competitive. Plus of course, riding is great physical conditioning. Here Williams F1 driver Alexander Albon (right) takes a few laps around the British Grand Prix Silverstone Circuit with his race engineer James Urwin prior to the 2022 race.

Another prerace driver/race engineer meeting. In this case Esteban Ocon, Alpine F1 team pilot, confers with Josh Peckett, Alpine F1 team race engineer, on the grid for the 2022 Austrian Grand Prix. Ocon finished a credible fifth that day, running a solid, points-earning race.

Number-One Mechanic

Head of the garage crew (informally known as "bolters" to F1 insiders), the number-one mechanic is responsible for the physical assembly and strip-down of the cars at the track (for logistical reasons the cars are shipped in pieces). They also maintain the cars and make the adjustments agreed by the driver and engineer.

Each driver's mechanics also act as his pit crew, a task that now requires greater physical fitness and agility than it did in the past, when the length of pit stops was dictated by refueling (now banned), meaning wheel changes could be more leisurely. All in all, this is one of F1's most grueling and unheralded jobs, although mechanics now work shorter hours than in previous years since the FIA instituted an overnight curfew for welfare reasons. The mechanics also generally fly economy, making them a hardy and resilient breed. They're also super-competitive (as this author discovered when joining the Red Bull crew for a five-a-side soccer game during a training week).

It has become a *Drive to Survive* storytelling trope that on-track incidents are generally followed by a cut to a reaction shot of the mechanics. That's partly because they're such a competitive bunch, partly because the arduousness of the job leaves them highly emotionally invested. It's in these reaction shots that you can tell how much respect the driver commands: When certain drivers throw their car off the road, the reaction is one of eye-rolling resignation rather than outrage or distress.

Such is the intensity of this job. Because of the many weekends away it entails, often mechanics succumb to the temptations of a factory-based role. Keen viewers may notice a missing face from the Red Bull garage reaction-shot menagerie in season 4: Max Verstappen's number-one mechanic Lee Stevenson, credited with superintending the rapid repair of Max's car ahead of the 2020 Hungarian GP, quit the traveling circus ahead of the 2021 season.

Mercedes F1's Chief Mechanic, Matt Deane, makes a point with his championship stallion Lewis Hamilton.

For logistical reasons, F1 cars are shipped to and from tracks in pieces. Here McLaren "bolters" work on a car in the Silverstone garages at the 2022 British Grand Prix.

In recent years Scuderia Ferrari pit stops generally fall into one of two categories: either slick and quick with minimal fault or delay or poorly strategized mistake-ridden affairs.

Physio

Where the race engineer fine-tunes the relationship between car and driver, with a side order of psychology, the physiotherapist, or physio, tunes up the driver's body—also with a bit of mind management on the side. Not for nothing do drivers often take their physio with them when they move teams: Like the relationship with the race engineer, this is a bond based on trust and mutual understanding, and on enabling the driver to access their own highest possible performance.

While many physios operating within F1 work for the Hintsa Performance company, some are sole operators and many have an eclectic history: Alexander Albon's performance coach Patrick Harding previously worked with the British canoeing squad at the Summer Olympics and trains the boxer Michael Conlan. Pyry Salmela, Pierre Gasly's Hintsa Performance physio, is a former ice hockey player.

Drive to Survive flourishes on drama and tension, so generally the physios appear in speaking roles when putting drivers through abstruse and painful-looking training processes or acting as part-time psychotherapist when times are hard. It wasn't always so: When Esteban Ocon first comes into focus in S1:E6, it suits the filmmakers to shoot him as a lone operator and outsider, training by himself. Later episodes embrace the relationships. There's a slightly awkward early meeting between Yuki Tsunoda and his performance coach Noel Carroll in a pub restaurant, in which Tsunoda is confused by his dish (the British staple of fish and chips with mushy peas); in the same episode (S4: E7), he's made to move house and go on a diet.

As Valtteri Bottas comes under pressure for his Mercedes seat by George Russell in 2021 (S4: E8), the scenes with physio Antti Vierula are as revealing as those with Valtteri's girlfriend, the cyclist Tiffany Cromwell. Here Vierula is not just a coach with a list of performance targets, he's effectively a driver whisperer as his charge's self-confidence crumbles before his eyes.

Serial World Champion Lewis Hamilton liberally credits his trainer/physiotherapist and all-around support system Angela Cullen for his unparalleled physical condition and success. Other than when he's in the car, you won't see these two more than a few feet apart at the racetrack.

Many have speculated that Angela Cullen
and Lewis Hamilton share a romantic
relationship, but it's simply not true
and both have become weary of this
unfounded speculation. Cullen is quite
happily married to her professional cyclist
husband and they are the parents of three
children. Technically she is Hamilton's
physiotherapist, but personal manager and
"right arm" might be better descriptions
as she is also in charge of Hamilton's
diet, sleeping habits, mental training,
and travel arrangements.

F1 Figures

Aki Hintsa

Human performance has been a recognized arbiter of success in F1 for decades, pioneered by Austrians Willi Dungl and Josef Leberer. But it was an orthopedic surgeon and former missionary from Finland who set what is now the accepted template for excellence. Aki Hintsa observed that "performance is a byproduct of well-being"

and developed a holistic method of training that encompassed both mind and body. Hintsa passed away in 2016 after a long battle with cancer, but the company he established still looks after the majority of the drivers on the F1 grid and his book, *The Core*, is required reading in the physio profession.

Physiotherapists, personal managers, and doctors are extremely important members of any F1 team. Aki Hintsa, McLaren team doctor (right) gives a few last prerace tips to 2009 F1 champion Jenson Button, at the 2011 Indian Grand Prix.

It's rare you'll see these two guys sitting next to each other at an official F1 press conference smiling and happy. Mercedes AMG Team Principal Toto Wolff (left) and his Red Bull counterpart Christian Horner (right) must, at some level, have certain respect for what the other has accomplished, yet it's always clear these guys just don't really like each other, as they are constantly verbally sparring and berating the other's opinion.

It's difficult to watch later series of *DTS* and *not* reach the conclusion that Toto Wolff lives rent-free in Christian Horner's head. The beef is deeply personal and cuts through the similarities between them: Both tried their hands at race driving before recognizing their talents lay elsewhere. Their lives diverged: Wolff going into the world of high finance before reentering motorsport as an investor/manager, Horner building his own race team.

While later episodes of S4 permit members of the Mercedes camp to suggest Horner's ire is motivated purely by jealousy of Wolff's success, it's more subtle than that. In S4: E1, Horner alludes to Wolff being "parachuted in" to a team that was already successful.

There's a compelling nugget of truth here. When Horner was recruited by Red Bull magnate Dietrich Mateschitz to run his team in 2005, Horner's Arden Racing organization were serial championship winners in F3000 (the precursor to today's Formula 2). Red Bull Racing wasn't a startup but an acquisition of a team that hadn't won anything in years and that required massive cultural change. Horner wasn't only responsible for poaching tech guru Adrian Newey from McLaren, he also retooled the team's culture, transforming them into the rabidly competitive fighting force that won four consecutive titles between 2010 and 2013.

Mercedes' team had a troubled history. Once owned by Honda, who pulled out of F1 during the global financial crisis of 2008, they had been forced to downsize and required greater investment than Mercedes anticipated. The board got nervous, and in early 2013 appointed Wolff and triple world champion Niki Lauda over the head of team principal Ross Brawn, who duly left. In 2014 the new hybrid power unit rules and Mercedes became dominant, largely due to Brawn's decision to invest early in the new engine technology.

Thus it's possible to argue Wolff inherited what was in effect a turn-key winning operation—although he's done a very good job of running it ever since . . .

RenaultSport's Cyril Abiteboul (left) with Gil DeFerran and Red Bull's Christian Horner at a Red Bull post-qualifying press conference. Abiteboul's days as a Red Bull engine provider were numbered as Horner was unhappy with the recent performance of the Renault engines, and also Renault's announcement of its intent to reenter F1 as a full factory team.

F1 Figures

What Happened to Cyril?

Drivers come and go and so to do key team personnel, especially at teams that answer to global corporations. Cyril Abiteboul, Christian Horner's nemesis in early seasons of *DTS* (Horner used to call him "Flav's tea boy" because Cyril came to F1 as an aide and paperwork wrangler to former Renault boss Flavio Briatore), frequently took a frontline role in *Drive to Survive* as the Renault team principal but was nowhere to be seen in season 4.

The team has had many owners and identities. Now under Renault ownership for a second time, they were run almost into the ground by their previous owners and needed more investment and more time to deliver on ambitions set out by the Renault board. As the figurehead, Abiteboul paid the political price and departed between the 2020 and 2021 seasons amid a wider shake-up of the Renault board and a rebranding of the team as Alpine (the car company's sporting subbrand).

The corporate restructure installed Laurent Rossi as president, Davide Brivio as sporting director, and former FIA man Marcin Budkowski as executive director. As an Abiteboul hire, Budkowski was always going to be out on a limb, and so it came to pass as he left in January 2022. You can read the tea leaves in S4: E7 when Laurent Rossi confidently introduces himself as the man holding the reins. Later in the episode, as Rossi and Brivio discuss Esteban Ocon's struggles, Budkowski is looking over from an adjoining table, excluded from the conversation. And, of course, it's Rossi who goes to the podium in Hungary to accept the trophy for winning constructor.

"Sometimes you win the race, and other times the race wins you." An unusual set of circumstances put young Alpine F1 talent Esteban Ocon atop the winner's podium, champagne bottle at the ready, as the seemingly unlikely winner of the 2021 Hungarian Grand Prix.

Chapter 2

HIGH-SPEED ART

A HISTORY OF F1 IN 20 CARS

State-of-the-art machinery is one of Formula 1's biggest draws: F1 offers the fastest, loudest, most technically advanced cars on the planet. Throughout F1's history, these cars have shaped the world and been shaped by it. Gasoline was still rationed in the UK when Britain hosted the first world championship grand prix in 1950, none of the cars had seat belts (it was believed to be better to be thrown out of the car in a crash rather than be stuck in the wreckage), and the commercial ecosystem of motor racing was primitive.

In this chapter we'll trace F1's journey to becoming one of the world's biggest television spectacles, and a multibillion-dollar business, by looking at a selection of these high-speed objects of automotive art. All of them were beautifully crafted to excel in their particular era, and all of them reflect the changing face of F1 and its inhabitants: manufacturers coming and going, tremendous feats of individual engineering ingenuity, and the making of heroes.

Ferrari weathered disappointing
results in 2020 and 2021 while
developing their 2022 car. Payback
came when that car, the F1-75,
proved competitive straightaway.

Alfa Romeo 158

As Europe rebuilt in the aftermath of World War II, motor racing began again, mostly with prewar cars that had escaped being melted down for munitions. The 158 dated back to 1936, first proposed by Enzo Ferrari when he was running Alfa Romeo's racing team. After the Italian surrender in 1943, the 158s were hidden from occupying forces so carefully that, come peacetime, it took months to locate them again. At least two had been concealed in a cheese factory.

To encourage as many entrants as possible, Europe's racing clubs agreed on shaping the technical rules of racing's top category (Formula A, later renamed Formula 1) around a format that allowed for supercharged 1.5-liter engines like those in the 158s as well as larger, unsupercharged engines. But Alfa almost missed out on competing in the inaugural world championship of 1950—it had pulled out of racing a year earlier after principal drivers Achille Varzi and Jean-Pierre Wimille were killed in accidents and third driver Count Carlo Felice Trossi, a chain smoker, died of cancer.

The prospect of the new world championship spurred Alfa's Italian dealer network to contribute to a sponsorship fund, which amassed 200 million lire, enough to pay for ongoing development and employ the best drivers of the day. Alfa Romeo proved unbeatable at first, but their grip gradually slipped as Enzo Ferrari's rival cars came on strong. Ferrari's naturally aspirated V-12 engines were less powerful but also less thirsty; in squeezing 420 brake horsepower from the little straight-eight engine, Alfa were getting little more than a mile per gallon by the end of 1951.

Age finally killed the 158s: The primitive chassis weren't up to handling more power and the engines were reaching the end of their working lives. Unwilling—or unable—to invest in F1's future, Alfa Romeo quit while they were (just about) ahead.

Giuseppe Farina (front) and Luigi Fagioli (back) battle it out in their Alfa Romeo 158s. Alfa Romeo dealers encouraged the company to reenter motorsports.

Driver Gear

The Crash Helmet

Like fighter pilots, early racing drivers preferred cloth caps and goggles to crash helmets—in case protective gear made people think they weren't made of the right stuff. Crash helmets became mandatory in 1952, but they remained basic: generally cork- or cotton-lined metal. U.S. manufacturer Bell introduced the first mass-made helmet with a laminated shell and absorbent foam liner, the 500-TX, in 1957.

Eleven years later, the first full-face helmets arrived, adapted from motorcycle racing. Although the look has remained similar, material and construction technology has evolved and F1 crash helmets now must meet ultratough safety standards. They are literally bulletproof.

Current Finnish driver Valtteri Bottas models a midcentury helmet design.

Argentine legend Juan Manuel Fangio seen at a vintage event in Long Beach, California, in 1976.

"HE COULD BE RUTHLESS, SWAPPING TEAMS AT SHORT NOTICE TO ENSURE HE GOT THE BEST CAR."

Arguably F1's first megastar, Juan Manuel Fangio was nearly thirty-nine when the world championship began. Many drivers of this generation had lost their best years to the war, but not this softly spoken Argentine—he still had what it took to win. Though a gentleman on- and off-track, he could be ruthless, swapping teams at short notice to ensure he got the best car. His record of five world titles stood for forty-eight years.

Mercedes W196

A new engine formula (maximum 2.5-liter naturally aspirated, 750cc supercharged) brought in for 1954 aimed to sweep away the prewar relics and encourage new manufacturer entries. It was transformative, pushing existing competitors to produce new designs and tempting Mercedes and Lancia to join the field.

Mercedes's W196 was technically advanced in almost every aspect, and even in those areas where it was merely on-trend, it set new standards. Mercedes wasn't alone in pivoting away from the primitive ladder-frame chassis design, but the W196's spaceframe design—a network of welded aluminum tubes—was rigorously stress-tested to ensure it combined optimal stiffness with minimal weight.

Having calculated that a supercharged engine would more than double the fuel consumption for a similar power output, Mercedes created a 2.5-liter unsupercharged straight-eight with high-pressure direct fuel injection and desmodronic valves (which close mechanically rather than relying on springs). Until this point, fuel injection had generally been used only in airplane engines.

Not only was the car class-leading, Mercedes raised the bar in trackside operations too. W196s rarely broke during races because they were so carefully built and maintained. When drivers came into the pits, a mechanic would be waiting with a drink and a wet towel—much appreciated in an era with a hot engine up front and drum brakes that spewed dust in the drivers' faces.

For tracks with long straights, Mercedes fitted special all-enclosed bodywork to reduce drag. First time out, at the French Grand Prix in 1954, the W196s of Juan Manuel Fangio and Karl Kling finished 1-2, a lap ahead of the third-place Ferrari. Rivals rushed to copy the idea but couldn't get it to work for them; these were early days in the science of automotive aerodynamics.

Few could compete with Mercedes, and it came as a relief to their rivals when they withdrew from motor racing at the end of 1955, stung by the public response to an accident during the 24 Hours of Le Mans race when one of their drivers crashed into the crowd.

Juan Manuel Fangio leads Stirling Moss in their class-leading W196s. The cars were technically advanced in almost every respect.

Cooper T51

Imagine being able to buy an F1 car in kit form to build yourself—or, if you didn't have all the equipment on hand, you could sweet-talk the manufacturer into letting you use a corner of their workshop or paying them to build it for you. In the 1950s this was a very real alternative to buying a complete car from, say, Maserati, or going cap-in-hand to Enzo Ferrari to see if you could rent one of his cars.

Now imagine if one of these kit racers actually won a grand prix and transformed motor racing in the process.

Founded in a London suburb in 1947 by Charles Cooper and his son John, the Cooper Car Company was one of those classic postwar British engineering businesses that began with someone tinkering in their garage.

Charles Cooper built his own car to go racing in 500cc Formula 3, and other competitors were so impressed they wanted to buy it from him. Within a handful of years, Cooper cars were competing in motor racing's highest categories.

What made Coopers different was where you would find the engine: in the back. While some prewar German grand prix cars had featured the engine behind the driver, in the 1950s F1 most cars were front-engined. It was practicality, not perversity, that dictated Cooper's approach: In 500cc racing, it had made sense to use a motorcycle engine and gearbox, and to keep the chain drive to the rear wheels. Having the engine behind the driver but ahead of the rear wheels made for better handling.

Cooper were still not taken seriously by the big manufacturers when they upscaled their F3 cars to F1—until Stirling Moss won the 1958 season-opening Argentine Grand Prix in a Cooper T43. Some thought this result a fluke, but a massive swing was coming. The following year Jack Brabham won the world championship in a Cooper, emphasizing that front-engined cars were now obsolete.

Not for the faint of heart. Jack Brabham expertly guides his Cooper T51 in first position at the 1959 Monaco Grand Prix.

Nicknamed "Black Jack" on account of his aggressive driving style—he'd put a wheel off-track to kick up stones in a chasing driver's face—Jack Brabham learned his trade in Australian dirt-track racing. A skilled mechanic, he was among the first drivers to have engineering input into a top-level race car: he got his break assembling Coopers and helped transform their F1 cars into winners. Brabham then set up his own company and became the first driver to win a grand prix, then the world championship, in a car bearing his own name.

Aussie Jack Brabham learned his craft of the dirt tracks of his home country.

" HE'D PUT A WHEEL OFF-TRACK TO KICK UP STONES IN A CHASING DRIVER'S FACE"

Ferrari 156

Spooked by rapidly increasing car performance, racing's governing body changed the rules to peg everybody back. Sound familiar? The storyline is almost as old as F1 itself.

Ahead of the 1961 season, the maximum engine size was slashed from 2.5 liters to 1.5. The decision was devastating to the British manufacturers, who had fought against the change and believed the battle won. None of them had an engine of suitable size ready to go.

Into this vacuum waltzed Ferrari. Two seasons had elapsed since the team last won the world championship as Enzo Ferrari grudgingly resisted F1's direction toward mid-engined cars. But for 1961 it would not only have a brand-new chassis, it had the perfect engine to go in it: a wide-angle V-6, developed from a concept already proven in the company's F2 cars.

In the long term, reducing engine size and power would force car makers to improve chassis performance (to conserve momentum through corners) and aerodynamics (to maximize speed in a straight line). But in this first year, the rug-pull handed the impetus to the team with the best engine, and Ferrari's 40-horsepower advantage made them the undoubted favorites.

Despite this, Ferrari didn't win the first race of the season. Stirling Moss, in an obsolete Lotus with a stopgap Coventry Climax straight-four engine, took a hard-fought victory on the streets of Monaco, keeping the Ferraris at bay over nearly 3 hours of racing. At times Moss was lapping nearly 3 seconds faster than his pole-position time. This is still considered to be one of the greatest grand prix drives of all.

At more open circuits, nothing could stand in Ferrari's way, and it became a question of which Maranello driver would win the world championship—a question answered in tragic circumstances with the death of Wolfgang von Trips in an accident at Monza.

A gorgeous "sharknose" Ferrari 156 tears through the Monaco circuit in 1962 with Phil Hill at the wheel.

In 1958 world champion Mike Hawthorn wore a shirt and jacket with a spotted bow tie. Overalls became obligatory in 1963, but it wasn't until 1975 that F1 adopted the fire-resistant material Nomex, originally used in spacesuits. U.S. safety pioneer Bill Simpson and NASA astronaut Pete Conrad, the third man to walk on the Moon, collaborated to make the first Nomex race suits and Simpson often demonstrated their benefits by setting himself on fire while wearing one. Like crash helmets, modern F1 race suits must comply with stringent standards—drivers even have to wear flameproof underwear.

"

SIMPSON OFTEN DEMONSTRATED THEIR BENEFITS BY SETTING HIMSELF ON FIRE"

Jackie Stewart (right) assists Graham Hill with repairs to his pre-Nomex race suit.

This photo, taken at the Dutch Grand Prix
in 1964, perfectly illustrates the simple
elegance of the Lotus 25. Peter Arundell
is in the driver's seat.

Formula 1 Drive to Survive: The Unofficial Companion

Lotus 25

Making a little engine power go a long way would become a key theme in the 1.5-liter era. Reducing the frontal area of cars to minimize air resistance and maximize straight-line speed was an obvious area of development, especially now that mid-mounted engines had become standard practice.

Compare a picture of a 1950s F1 car with one from the 1960s and you'll notice immediately how the driver of the later car is almost lying down rather than sitting upright. This change required a new way of building the car—it simply wasn't possible to make a conventional multitube spaceframe structure strong and small enough while accommodating a driver at such an extreme angle.

Legend has it that visionary engineer Colin Chapman drew the first sketches of what would become the Lotus 25 on a restaurant napkin while waiting for his lunch. Chapman had founded his company in a garage under a railway arch in North London and built a reputation for making fast and light, if often fragile, racing cars. With the Lotus 25 he would achieve the engineering holy grail of making a single element of the car perform more than one task: Where conventional race cars had bodywork fitted to a separate steel chassis frame, in Chapman's new Lotus the "skin" would also be a load-bearing element of the structure. This monocoque concept saved weight and allowed the driver to sit in an aero-optimal position.

As Lotus's race team racked up pole positions and victories, customers of the now-obsolete Lotus 24, who had been assured the new car would be mechanically identical, were left frustrated. But so it was with Chapman, a man as slippery and ruthless in business as he was inspired at the drawing board.

Drivers were delighted when motorsport regulators doubled the maximum displacement for 1966. The engine manufacturers, mostly caught by surprise again, were less happy. But once again, change prompted an innovation that would change F1 forever.

Lotus impresario Colin Chapman, with the collaboration of Ford UK PR man Walter Hayes, managed to whistle £100,000 from the Ford Motor Company to underwrite a four-cylinder twin-cam engine for F2 and a three-liter V-8 for F1, both developed by the Cosworth company. Hayes was confident enough to assure Henry Ford II himself the V-8 was "fairly likely" to win a world championship. It would win many more than one.

Although Lotus had pioneered monocoque chassis construction with the Type 25, and others had followed, they still required some form of bracing around the engine and gearbox to transfer suspension loads. Cosworth's DFV V-8 was designed to be strong enough to accept such forces and bolt straight to the main element of the car, saving further weight.

When the Type 49 rolled off the truck at Zandvoort for the Dutch Grand Prix, the third round of the 1967 season, rivals instantly identified it as a game-changer. In the hands of Jim Clark, the peerless driver of the era, it was stoppable only by the unreliability that tended to plague Lotuses.

The Type 49 also was notable for being the first leading F1 car to feature prominent tobacco sponsorship. Since the earliest days of motor racing, entrants had run in so-called national colors—green for Britain—so traditionalists greeted Lotus's adoption of red-and-gold Player's Tobacco imagery with fury. At a non-championship race at Brands Hatch in 1968, Graham Hill was ordered to leave the track so the logo on his car could be taped over.

Lotus also began to add airfoils to the front and rear of the 49 to boost cornering speeds. They were primitive, fragile, and quickly banned, but they began the transition to the car shapes we recognize today.

This view of the Lotus 49 in 1968 offers a good look at its fragile front airfoils and then controversial Player's Tobacco livery. Graham Hill is in the cockpit.

The first British driver to become a tax exile on account of his earnings, Clark was brilliant in whatever car he drove. This was an era in which drivers were paid per race, so they might be seen in a touring car one week and a grand prix the next, or even in the support races for an F1 event. Clark even led the Indy 500, but he was eliminated by mechanical trouble. He might have won more than two world championships and certainly more races, but for car failures. The cause of his fatal accident in a Formula 2 race in Germany never has been definitively explained.

"

CLARK WAS BRILLIANT IN WHATEVER CAR HE DROVE."

Jim Clark takes a break at West Germany's Nürburgring in 1961.

Tyrrell 001

Ken Tyrrell was a timber merchant with a taste for racing, and his team graduated from the lower ranks of single-seater competition to be F1 contenders in partnership with Matra, an aerospace company with a sideline in sports cars. However, Matra's acquisition by the French division of Chrysler in 1969 meant it would no longer be politically possible to use the Ford-badged Cosworth V-8. Matra had a V-12. Yet when star driver Jackie Stewart tested it, he said that while it made a nice noise, they would never win a world championship with it.

Sticking with the Ford engine meant an end to the Matra partnership—and, while McLaren, Brabham, and Lotus had lucrative businesses selling cars to other teams, all of them ruled out supplying a direct competitor. This was an era in which F1 was overtaking sportscar racing in the public consciousness, races were being broadcast on TV more often, and the rewards were greater and the political pressures more intense.

So Ken Tyrrell concluded a secret deal with a little-known engineer, Derek Gardner, whose sole involvement in F1 had been to work on a four-wheel-drive transmission system Tyrrell had tested before the concept was banned. Gardner had never designed a car before, so he based his work on photographs and intuition, building a mockup in his garage from wood, chicken wire, and cardboard. An engine and gearbox were driven to his house under cover of darkness to assess the fit, and Stewart also paid a clandestine visit so the cockpit could be tailored to him. When the design was ready, the metal panels were sourced from the company that built the titular car for the movie *Chitty Chitty Bang Bang*.

While the 001 saw action in just a handful of races, it provided a stepping-stone to cars that would enable Stewart to add two world titles to his honors—and showed how individual ingenuity could still trump a large R&D budget.

While the Tyrrell 001 was campaigned in just a handful of races, the concepts employed by engineer Derek Gardner were stepping-stones to later designs.

The Lotus 72's wedge shape was a radical departure from the cigar-shaped race cars that preceded it. Here Jochen Rindt puts a 72 through its paces at the 1970 Spanish Grand Prix.

There is no such thing as a level playing field in F1. Given enough leeway, cunning engineers will find a way to establish a competitive edge by means fair or foul. Sometimes that buccaneering spirit overreaches and has to be reined in.

Although Lotus had facilitated the deal to create the Ford-Cosworth DFV V-8, they only enjoyed exclusivity on it for a year—1967—and from then on it was available to everyone. If the majority of the grid had equal engine power, that meant having to look elsewhere for the "unfair advantage."

Lotus's wedge-shaped Type 72 marked the transition from the cigar-shaped designs that had dominated the grid for decades to the wedgy, aerodynamically optimized

shapes, which would define F1's future. Designers Colin Chapman and Maurice Phillippe moved the radiators from their traditional location at the front of the car to a position just ahead of the rear wheels, enabling the nose to be lower and flatter. It also shifted weight toward the rear, useful for improving traction at a time when engine power exceeded tire grip.

The 72 bristled with other ambitious engineering, including rising-rate suspension—so-called because it was set up to increase resistance as it moved through its available travel—using torsion bars rather than springs, also enabling the front bodywork to be very slim. But it was all too much at once. The suspension geometry was designed to resist

the tendency of the nose to dive under braking and the rear to squat under acceleration, but this came at a cost of driver "feel"—and lap times.

Unveiled early in 1970, the 72 was withdrawn for a hasty redesign and not reintroduced until round five of the championship, the Dutch Grand Prix, which Lotus's Jochen Rindt won by a 30 second margin. Rindt won the next three races and then was killed in a crash during qualifying for the Italian Grand Prix when a front brake shaft snapped. He remains the only posthumous world champion.

Renault RS01

In 2017 the Renault Formula 1 team celebrated the fortieth anniversary of its debut by releasing an unusual limited-edition merchandise item: a chic, angular, bright yellow and black $195 electric kettle. The passage of time had enabled the organization to laugh at its own expense. Renault's RS01 car was groundbreaking but ultimately a brave failure, cruelly dubbed "the yellow teapot" by rivals on account of its tendency to expire in a cloud of smoke.

When the RS01 appeared for the first time at the 1977 British Grand Prix weekend, it was an outlier, the first car to take advantage of rules permitting 1.5-liter turbocharged engines. Of the twenty-nine other cars starting the race, all but five were powered by Ford-Cosworth V-8s. Ferrari's flat-twelve was the only competitive non-Ford engine available.

Since the RS01 was in effect a mobile testbed—with driver Jean-Pierre Jabouille as chief engineer—its significance flew under the radar. Yes, it was clunky and overweight, and its turbocharged engine and new Michelin radial tires were untried in competition. The crudity of the chassis meant other competitors were slow to pick up on the significant advance those radials represented over the cross-ply Goodyears everyone else was using.

In the coming years radial tires would become ubiquitous—as would turbocharged engines. As Renault conquered the reliability and drivability problems—the first iteration suffered a massive lag in acceleration as the turbo spooled up—rivals who had laughed whenever the RS01 stopped in a haze of gray fog realized they were being left behind. Come the early 1980s, if you didn't have a turbo engine, you were lost.

> ## " COME THE EARLY 1980S, IF YOU DIDN'T HAVE A TURBO ENGINE YOU WERE LOST. "

No reprieve for weather. The much-maligned Renault RS01 is seen before retiring with a broken alternator at the 1977 U.S. Grand Prix at Watkins Glen.

What many people don't understand about aerodynamics is that it's essentially a process of manipulating suction. The difference in speed between the air flowing under and over a wing generates negative pressure: Airplane wings suck the plane upward; race car wings suck the vehicle downward.

Although F1 cars had been sporting various forms of airfoils since 1968, the science was in its infancy and the next step forward would come as the result of a happy accident. In the mid-1970s Lotus set up an R&D group to work on a car, which would in effect have a giant wing. Engineer Peter Wright spent many hours in the wind tunnel evaluating side-mounted wing and radiator combinations with a balsawood model. One day the aging model began to sag, generating peculiar results. Wright realized that sealing the gap between the sidepod edges and the road surface was the key to boosting the suction effect.

Converting this discovery into an effective race car would take months more research into the best way to achieve a seal, and the first Lotus wing car—the Type 78—was only a qualified success. The center of pressure was too far forward, requiring a large rear wing to balance it. Lotus remedied this with the Type 79, which ushered in the new era of what became known as "ground effect."

Mario Andretti claimed five wins in the 79 on his way to winning the world championship in 1978, but the car wasn't without its problems: Making the chassis narrow, to maximize the aerodynamic effect of the sidepods, caused structural weaknesses and the inboard rear brakes were prone to overheating. Others would do ground effect better by allying it to more rigid chassis, but the Lotus 79 remains the iconic and genre-defining wing car.

Jean-Pierre Jarier drives a Lotus 79 at Watkins Glen in 1978.

It's remarkable to think Mario Andretti remains the last American driver to win the F1 world championship. Italian-born, Andretti emigrated to the United States with his family as a child and got a fake ID to enter his first car race when he was underage. Beginning in dirt-track racing, Andretti honed skills that would make him a winner in NASCAR, IndyCar, and sportscars, as well as F1.

Mario Andretti celebrates victory at the United States Grand Prix West in Long Beach, California, on April 3, 1977.

 MARIO ANDRETTI REMAINS THE LAST AMERICAN DRIVER TO WIN THE F1 WORLD CHAMPIONSHIP."

McLaren MP4/1

Today every car on the F1 grid is made from carbon fiber. But when McLaren first drew up plans for a car with a composite structure, the idea was viewed as fringe science. Other teams had taken advantage of carbon fiber's lightweight properties on small, nonstructural components, but the key objection to building a complete car with it was that nobody knew what would happen in a crash. Might it not just explode in a shower of dust and shards?

John Barnard, McLaren's single-minded chief designer, was new to the job after spending time on the U.S. racing scene, where he felt there was much more of a can-do culture. He pursued his carbon-car project with almost messianic determination. It would be, quite literally, rocket science: McLaren and their suppliers had plenty of expertise in the folded metal structures that made up a traditional F1's car's monocoque chassis, but no facilities to work with composite materials. That search took them to Hercules Aerospace in Utah, the company that built, among other things, the solid-fuel rocket motors for Polaris missiles and the boosters for the Titan rockets used to launch the *Voyager* deep-space probes.

McLaren had been in a competitive slump for three years, bad enough for title sponsor Marlboro to push for the change of management, which brought Barnard on board. Introduced in the third race of the 1981 season, the MP4/1 took its first podium finish four races later and John Watson claimed its first victory in the British Grand Prix.

This 1981 photo taken behind Silverstone's pit wall offers a good inside view of the McLaren MP4/1's ground-breaking carbon-fiber construction.

Formula 1 Drive to Survive: The Unofficial Companion

Brabham BT52

Although many F1 fans believe the Brabham BT53 to be among the most beautiful racing cars of all time, it was a pure case of form following function—there was no time to consider aesthetics.

The early 1980s was a time of ugly political rancor in F1. Motor racing's governing body faced off against the Formula One Constructors' Association (FOCA) and the battle lines were drawn, not for the first or last time, over technical regulations and money. Brabham owner Bernie Ecclestone was a key player in FOCA and was keen to expand his influence in F1's financial affairs.

Against this febrile background the governing body had been trying—with mixed results—to contain the performance gains teams were finding by combining ground effect aerodynamics with increasingly powerful turbocharged engines. In 1982 two drivers were killed in accidents and another suffered life-changing injuries.

Among the proposals for 1983 were flat-bottomed cars—to eliminate ground effect—and smaller fuel tanks. Ecclestone assured his chief designer, the exceptionally creative Gordon Murray, that flat bottoms wouldn't happen. But, seeing the bigger picture of compromise, Ecclestone eventually caved on that point. Murray, like many of his rivals, had to tear up the designs for his 1983 car.

Working long hours and fueled by amphetamines, Murray and his tiny team of engineers rushed out a new car in just six weeks. It was slim, stiff, and had a tiny fuel tank—Murray worked that the time gained by running lighter would trade off favorably against time lost by stopping for more fuel.

Nelson Piquet pilots the Brabham BT52 at
United States Grand Prix West in Long Beach,
California, March 25–27, 1983.

McLaren MP4/4

By 1987 Honda's turbo engines had achieved such a position of dominance that the FIA thought it was doing the other competitors in F1 a favor by announcing a ban on turbos for the 1989 season and cutting boost levels (from 4 bar to 2.5) and fuel tank capacity (from 195 liters to 150) for 1988. FIA President Jean-Marie Balestre confidently announced no turbo car could win a race in '88.

Instead Honda doubled down with the encouragement of their new partner, McLaren, making an all-new engine to suit the new rules in the last year of turbos.

McLaren's 1988 car, the MP4/4, was also all-new and a work of art. Designed by Steve Nichols and new technical director Gordon Murray, the car featured a low-line body style to reduce drag, an unusual look in an era when turbo power had prompted cars to sprout huge wings. It was a truly collaborative car in that Honda designed their engine with a lower crankshaft to maximize the potential of the low-profile design concept.

The MP4/4's late completion, just weeks before the start of the season, meant McLaren's competitors received little notice of what was to come. Alain Prost won the season-opening Brazilian Grand Prix from pole position by 10 seconds despite slowing down to save fuel in the final laps. Next time out, in Imola, Prost's new teammate, Ayrton Senna, also won from pole. Senna's qualifying lap was over 3 seconds faster than the third-place car and the McLarens finished a lap ahead of anybody else.

Only in Italy, when Prost retired and Senna tangled with a back marker, was McLaren's superiority broken. The only question was which of the two drivers would win the drivers' title—an issue that generated the first rumblings of what would become one of the greatest rivalries of all time.

McLaren's 1988 car, the MP4/4, driven here by Alain Prost, featured a low-line body style to reduce drag, an unusual look in at the time.

Great Drivers

Ayrton Senna

Brazil has a rich history of producing incredibly competitive racing drivers, but undoubtedly the greatest was Ayrton Senna. A brooding, complicated, brilliant, often difficult individual, he was both quick and ruthless. If you saw his yellow crash helmet in your mirrors, you got out of the way. His uncompromising nature led him to clash with teammates, team bosses, and FIA leaders. His tragic death during the 1994 San Marino Grand Prix changed motor racing forever.

A brooding Ayrton Senna adjusts the mirror of his Lotus 98T in 1986.

" UNDOUBTEDLY THE GREATEST WAS AYRTON SENNA"

Ferrari 640

Ferrari is synonymous with the glamour, sophistication, and high performance. It's inextricably associated, too, with poisonous internal politics—a habit ingrained since the days of Enzo Ferrari himself, a believer in creative tension and a self-confessed "agitator of men."

In his waning years, Enzo grew frustrated by his team's patchy form and concluded a deal to bring star designer John Barnard over from McLaren, a decision met with dismay by company loyalists. So desperate was Ferrari to secure Barnard's services that Enzo agreed to let his new recruit stay in England and set up a new design HQ near his home in Godalming.

Barnard's next big idea was to eliminate the mechanical shifting mechanism of the gearbox and manage it electronically so the drivers could change gear without taking their hands off the steering wheel. But progress on his new car was inexplicably delayed. Eventually Barnard found out what was going on: A faction led by Enzo's illegitimate son Piero was using Maranello's resources to design its own car.

Enzo passed away in late summer 1988, but not before he'd sent his own son into exile elsewhere in the company and empowered Barnard to press on. Arriving a year later than hoped, the new car was troubled—crankshaft vibrations kept throwing the alternator belt off and making the gearbox shut down—but it won its first race.

The semiautomatic gearshift is now standard in F1 and a 641—Ferrari's 1990 follow-up—hangs in the New York Museum of Modern Art.

Nigel Mansell drives a Ferrari 640. The car was developed under much palace intrigue.

Williams FW14B

Drive to Survive viewers have seen Williams at their lowest ebb, but this team once defined technical excellence and pugnacious British grit. With the FW14B, Williams harnessed experimental technologies other teams had tried and abandoned. The result was a period of frenzied competitiveness that prompted yet another FIA clampdown to control car performance.

The original FW14 of 1991 was the first Williams to feature input from Adrian Newey, a visionary designer who combined aerodynamic expertise with hands-on race engineering experience gleaned from working with Bobby Rahal in IndyCar racing. Newey cars are characterized by zero-compromise aerodynamics: Drivers love the performance but dislike the cramped cockpit environment. The FW14 featured Newey touches such as a raised nose cone, which encouraged airflow under the car toward the diffuser under the gearbox. Its Renault V-10 also bristled with the latest technology, including pneumatic valves. In the B-spec car introduced for 1992, Williams added active suspension and traction control to an electronics package that already featured a semiautomatic gearbox.

Active suspension wasn't there to make the car more comfortable. Its purpose was to keep the FW14B perfectly flat relative to the track surface so its aerodynamics would function at maximum efficiency. But this required a certain kind of driver. The system robbed the driver of steering "feel," so they just had to trust that it would work. The abnormally brave Nigel Mansell had that faith and confidence; teammate Riccardo Patrese didn't. Having been comparable all through 1991, the following season Patrese simply couldn't keep up with Mansell.

Cars such as the FW14B posed philosophical questions as well as raising issues of safety. Should the best drivers in the world be given this much technological help? The answer, then and now, is no.

Driver Gear

The Gloves

Driving gloves date to the earliest days of the automobile, when steering wheels were made of wood or metal and often slippery. Gloves were practical as well as stylish. Now they fulfill an important safety function as well and are subject to the same fireproofing regulations as the rest of the driver's attire. Although there's room for customization (some drivers prefer the seams to be outside rather than inside), F1 gloves also have to feature biometric sensors, which transmit the driver's pulse rate and the amount of oxygen in their blood over an encrypted Bluetooth connection.

Nikita Mazepin adjusts his gloves prior to competition. Today's gloves feature biometric sensors.

Ferrari F2004

The greatest F1 car ever? Michael Schumacher recovers his Ferrari F2004 from a spin in qualifying at the 2004 Silverstone race.

What is the greatest ever F1 car? Ferrari's F2004 has a strong case: It took twenty-nine podium finishes, including fifteen wins, plus twelve pole positions and fourteen fastest laps, and it still holds the outright lap record at several circuits, including Monza, the temple of speed. It propelled Michael Schumacher to his record-breaking seventh world championship and enabled him to surpass his previous record for consecutive victories and wins within a season. By the thirteenth of the eighteen races in 2004, Ferrari had secured the constructors' championship and the only other person mathematically in contention for the drivers' title was Schumacher's teammate Rubens Barrichello.

It was not a year that would have made a thrilling season of *Drive to Survive*, since the Ferrari regime at the time wouldn't have let the cameras in. Under Jean Todt's leadership, the team had become a relentless winning machine. Hiring Schumacher in 1996 had been the tipping point: Already a double world champion, he attracted some of the best engineers in the business and Todt shielded the team's personnel from the worst excesses of the Italian media and politics elsewhere in the Ferrari empire. From 2000 to 2004, Michael was pretty much unbeatable, rarely more so than in '04 when the F2004 excelled and key rivals stumbled. The car proved so

quick at its first test—almost 2 seconds a lap faster than its predecessor—that Ferrari themselves were baffled.

While this era is fondly remembered by Ferrari fans, it was a period of intense political turmoil, intrigue over cheating (a ban on traction-control systems was abandoned when it proved impossible to enforce), and heavy-handed rule-tinkering by the FIA as it came under pressure to curb Ferrari's superiority.

Believe it or not, there was a time when very few people had heard of Michael Schumacher—not least financially troubled F1 team boss Eddie Jordan, who in 1991 had debts to pay and a seat to fill (the vacancy was caused by his driver, Bertrand Gachot, being jailed for spraying a London taxi driver with CS gas in a road rage incident). Faced with a choice of several drivers, Jordan took the one who was bringing $150,000 in cash from Mercedes. The rest is history: Schumacher reset the boundaries of what was expected from drivers in terms of professionalism and physical fitness as well as speed, winning seven world titles.

SCHUMACHER RESET THE BOUNDARIES OF WHAT WAS EXPECTED FROM DRIVERS"

Michael Schumacher celebrates a win at the Hungarian Grand Prix, on August 15, 2004.

McLaren's rivalry with Ferrari has lain dormant for a decade, but at its most intense it was even more toxic than the Red Bull–Mercedes rancor, which has entertained fans in recent seasons of *Drive to Survive*. No other F1 car has been conceived, built, and raced in such poisonous circumstances as McLaren's MP4-23, the car in which Lewis Hamilton claimed his first world title by a single point—with an overtaking move on the last corner of the last lap of the final grand prix of the year.

Hamilton's debut season, 2007, had been marred by infighting with his teammate, Fernando Alonso, and ended with Alonso leaving after just one year with the team—but not before he'd played a part in a bigger scandal. McLaren's chief designer had obtained design schematics from a disgruntled Ferrari employee, their aim being to find better jobs elsewhere and quietly use the information to make themselves look smarter. But once this was exposed, the course of events—a prolonged drip of revelations, accusations, denial, and counteraccusations between the two teams—meant questions were rightly asked about how many people within McLaren knew of the theft. The team was fined an incredible $100 million, and the designs of the 2008 car, the MP4-23, were forensically examined for traces of Ferrari methodology.

Hamilton was already a media sensation thanks to his story, his driving talent, and the fact that he'd taken the championship battle to the wire in his maiden season. Now it was tough to get a seat in the press room, such was the mass-market interest in his fortunes.

In the bigger picture, questions were also being raised about the aerodynamic complexity of F1 cars and how it worked against overtaking. Newer, simpler cars with mild hybrid electrical boost were mandated for 2009—so it's ironic that F1's ultimate aero era should have closed with Hamilton's thrilling last-gasp championship victory.

> **"NO OTHER F1 CAR HAS BEEN CONCEIVED, BUILT, AND RACED IN SUCH POISONOUS CIRCUMSTANCES AS MCLAREN'S MP4-23"**

The pit crew struggles with a front wheel on Lewis Hamilton's McLaren MP4-23 at the 2008 Malaysian Grand Prix.

Red Bull RB9

Fiddling with the rules, even in a well-intentioned way, often has unintended consequences. During the 2000s the FIA, led by the autocratic Max Mosley, brought in a succession of changes aimed at cutting costs for competitors (or preventing them from spending too much) and improving overtaking opportunities. These measures included banning exotic materials from engines, mandating that engines and

gearboxes had to last more than one race, downsizing engines from 3.0-liter V-10s to 2.4-liter V-8s, decreasing the permitted rev limit, standardizing electronic systems to prevent teams using traction control, and mandating simplified aerodynamics. Somehow the biggest spenders with the best engineers found their way around these restrictions to become virtually unbeatable.

Red Bull's RB9 was the last in a line of such cars that delivered Sebastian Vettel to four consecutive world championships from 2010 to 2013. A key weapon in Red Bull's armory was their close relationship with Renault—though *Drive to Survive* fans will recall that this didn't end well. Back when the partners got along, Renault developed some very clever engine mapping that enabled Red Bull to use exhaust

gases to boost aerodynamic performance. The FIA tried to close this off, feeling that the technique—which used extra fuel that was then burned in the exhaust pipe—didn't send out a positive environmental message.

Whatever the FIA tried, Red Bull found a way around it. On the RB9, for instance, the sloping "Coanda" exhaust ramp neutralized a new regulation on where the exhaust exit could be sited. The car produced so much aerodynamic downforce it was often too hard on its tires, but here Red Bull got lucky. After several tire failures in the British Grand Prix, Pirelli reverted to a previous stronger construction type, and Vettel broke the record for consecutive wins in a season.

Mark Webber negotiates his Red Bull RB9 through the start of the Belgian Grand Prix at Spa-Francorchamps on August 25, 2013.

Mercedes F1 W05

When Jean Todt took over from Max Mosley as FIA president, one of the pressing issues he felt he had to tackle was F1's image as a gas-guzzling sport, increasingly out of step with audience tastes and the direction of the wider automotive industry. This was a looming existential crisis, since F1 depends on manufacturer involvement—and high-profile companies such as Renault, which had made big bets on EVs, were warning that unless F1 reflected the road cars they were actually making, what was the point?

2013 was the year set for a new engine formula that would embrace downsizing and electrification. That slipped to 2014 as arguments raged over the details. Very quietly Mercedes, which had returned as a manufacturer team in 2010, had its engine division channel resources into researching the best solutions and identifying likely problems.

Finally, the stakeholders agreed on a package of 1.6-liter turbocharged hybrid V-6s with limits on revs, how much fuel could be used in a race, and how much fuel could flow at any given time. The hybrid systems were complex, including energy recovery from the brakes and exhaust, and another that could use recovered energy to make the turbo spin, reducing the lag that is a hallmark of turbocharging. This element proved most problematic because the rotational speed of a turbo (up to 200,000 rpm) poses huge challenges for lubrication and heat management. Mercedes solved it first, giving them a lasting advantage through the first five seasons of the hybrid era. By contrast Renault did a poor job, causing the schism with Red Bull that Netflix viewers will recall.

Commercial rights holder Bernie Ecclestone hated the Mercedes dominance that ensued (the F1 W05 won sixteen out of nineteen races) and imposed a kneejerk rule change to spice things up, awarding double points in the season finale. He loathed the quietness of the engines relative to the V-8s too, hence further changes were to come.

F1 head Bernie Ecclestone detested the dominance of the Mercedes F1 W05. Lewis Hamilton drives his W05 in qualifying for the Singapore Grand Prix on September 20, 2014.

![Helmet icon] **Driver Gear**

The Watch

It was Jackie Stewart who first caught on to the importance of watches to a driver. Recognizing the possibility of losing skin—or worse—in an accident if his watch was ripped from his wrist (known as "de-gloving"), Stewart liked to make a point of handing his watch over to team boss Ken Tyrrell for safekeeping while he was on track. Since Stewart already had a sponsorship arrangement with Rolex, this little piece of theater made for a handy marketing gimmick—indeed, well over four decades after his retirement, Stewart remained a fixture in the F1 paddock hosting Rolex VIPs. In recent years, teams and drivers have been keen to strike deals with other high-end watchmakers and have gotten around the bans on wearing them by stitching replica patterns into their suits and gloves.

Jackie Stewart (right) and driver Mark Webber compare Rolexes at the 2004 Chinese Grand Prix.

When Liberty Media acquired the commercial rights to F1 in 2017 and immediately parked former "ringmaster" Bernie Ecclestone in a non-job ("chairman emeritus"), fresh air whistled through the paddock. Now a company that understood the modern audience was in charge rather than an individual whose idea of entertainment was solidly rooted in the last century.

As well as granting unprecedented access to Box to Box productions to make *Drive to Survive* (a course correction so drastic that Mercedes and Ferrari declined to participate in season 1), Liberty laid out plans to add pizzazz to each event and to improve the on-track spectacle. Clearly this last ambition was something that had been attempted many times before, generally ending in failure.

To maximize the chances of success this time around, Liberty engaged an entire department of engineers with long F1 experience to work on a new set of technical regulations that would enable cars to follow each other closely enough to overtake. This group had seen enough rule changes in their time to be aware of the potential for unintended consequences—and to avoid them.

The result was the great reset of 2022. This new generation of cars is less reliant on their front and rear wings for cornering performance, and less disruptive to cars behind.

Ferrari's own recent problems will be familiar to viewers. Through 2020 and 2021, they chose to focus their development resources on their 2022 package in the hope of establishing an advantage. Payback came when the F1-75 proved competitive straightaway.

Unlike Mercedes, Ferrari had successfully navigated some of the potential pitfalls of the new formula. Their car was competitive and looked fantastic. But after Charles Leclerc carved out an early lead in the drivers' championship Ferrari, as so often in the past, things went into self-destruct mode: engine failures and strategic blunders compounded mistakes by the drivers themselves.

It all made for an entertaining spectacle—just as F1's new owners had hoped.

" NOW A COMPANY THAT UNDERSTOOD THE MODERN AUDIENCE WAS IN CHARGE"

Carlos Sainz's Ferrari F1-75 is seen in a moment of repose at the 2022 Australian Grand Prix.

Chapter 3

THE SCIENCE OF SPEED

F1 TECHNOLOGY

While the drivers take top billing, the cars they race and the teams that design, build, and operate those cars are the keys to success. When you cut F1 down to its essence, it's about getting a car to cover a set distance in the shortest possible time. By all means, hire the fastest driver, but they need a cast of hundreds of experts to get them to the checkered flag first.

The somewhat exaggerated blur of Zhou Guanyu's 2022 Ferrari-powered Alfa Romeo isn't so far from the truth of the speed and aerodynamic forces at work. Modern F1 performance is a dizzying combination of power, aerodynamics, electronics, suspension, computer-aided design, and oh yeah, let's not forget a supremely talented driver.

In the Beginning

Except for featuring cars with four wheels, the first races to carry the name "grand prix" would be barely recognizable as such to fans of *Drive to Survive*. These were timed events on public roads in which competitors set off at intervals, racing against the clock as much as each other. And by "competitors" we mean individual drivers *and* "riding mechanics" who stayed on board to fix the car if something went wrong—which it often did. Racing cars of the day were neither sophisticated nor fast by today's standards.

The first grand prix, held in France in 1906, was won by the Hungarian Ferenc Szisz and held over a 64.1-mile lap, which entrants had to cover a total of twelve times over the course of a hot midsummer weekend. Szisz's Renault car was a bespoke racing machine with a 13-liter four-cylinder engine producing 90 brake horsepower at a heady 1,200 rpm, driving the rear wheels via a three-speed

Ferenc Szisz sits behind the wheel of his
purpose-built Renault, with which he won the
first grand prix in 1906.

The light, lithe Bugatti 35 was the seminal
Grand Prix car of the 1920s, moving the
science of Grand Prix car design from its
near Stone Age beginnings and into the
1930s. This dramatic shot was captured at
an Italian Grand Prix event at Garda, 1926.

manual gearbox, and was clocked at a maximum speed of 96 miles per hour. If this velocity seems humble, bear in mind the only braking systems were a foot-operated metal band, which squeezed the gearbox shaft, and a pair of drums on the rear wheels, which Szisz had to activate by pulling a lever.

But even in this primitive era, just as today, winning came down to strategic decisions in design and race execution. The rules in the 1906 French GP capped car weight at 1,000 kilograms, difficult to achieve given the size of the engine required. Michelin had new tires available on detachable rims, which meant the driver and mechanic could change tires in 4 minutes rather than 10, but at a cost of heavier wheels. Renault opted to run these, but only on the back axle's more

highly stressed drive wheels and the team did a precautionary change every two laps. To save weight, they also removed the differential (a set of gears that allows the outside rear wheel to spin faster than the inner wheel through turns)—theoretically an impediment to cornering performance, but not such a problem on a long triangular course with only three sharp bends. Szisz's 32 minute margin of victory owed much to the fact that his car was the fastest in a straight line and spent less time being worked on.

This charming archival photo of the 1931 Monaco Grand Prix gives an idea of how straightforward, if not downright basic, a sports car, and sports racing machine was all those days ago. Not a wing to be found, tall skinny tires, and the car's electrics likely consisted of little more than a battery, magneto, spark plugs and a simple ignition system.

In the early days, Enzo Ferrari nearly always attended F1 races with his team, seen here wearing his trademark dark glasses, dress shirt, suspenders, and tie. In later years when closed-circuit TV was becoming prevelant, he'd often stay in his office and watch the action from a distance.

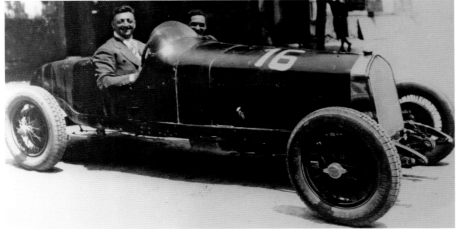

Enzo Ferrari had considerable chops as a racing car driver, which enabled him to become a superb Alfa Romeo racing team manager and entrant, and ultimately a car builder and the supreme force in Formula 1. This 1927 shot shows him aboard an Alfa GP racer.

Midcentury Modern

While the drivers have rightly become the stars of the show since the days of poor old Szisz (Renault pocketed the entire 45,000-Franc prize), technology and teamwork are what have put them on the stage.

When the F1 world championship began in 1950, the cars ran on spindly cross-ply tires, aerodynamics were barely understood, and there were no safety features as such (not even seatbelts—it was believed to be better for the driver to be thrown from the car if it crashed, in case it caught fire). Just a handful of people were responsible for designing, building, and operating the race cars.

Competition drove innovations such as independent suspension, disc brakes, fuel-injected engines, radial tires, semiautomatic seamless-shift gearboxes, and advanced chassis construction. The first F1 cars had the engine in front of the driver, and the chassis—essentially the car's underlying skeleton—was a simple ladderlike frame with bodywork bolted or riveted on top. Moving the engine behind the driver in the late 1950s improved car balance, and smarter chassis construction made the cars lighter and faster: ladder frames evolved into spaceframes, a network of carefully stress-tested tubes; then the monocoque principle enabled engineers to use the outer skin of the car to absorb chassis loads rather than functioning as mere decoration. Aerodynamics became another key arbiter of performance and could boost cornering speeds as well as improve the straight-line figures.

Like the Bugatti 35 that came before it, this Mercedes-Benz W196 rewrote the standard and the history books of Formula 1. It competed in the 1954 and 1955 F1 seasons, and its shrieking 2.5-liter inline-eight used highly advanced technology putting out prodigious power. The W196's track record was impressive indeed: nine victories and fastest laps, as well as eight pole positions in the twelve Grand Prix races in which it was entered, and, of course, Fangio's world champion's titles in 1954 and 1955.

"THE DRIVERS HAVE RIGHTLY BECOME THE STARS OF THE SHOW"

The bull-chested Argentine Jose Froilan Gonzalez (notable for winning Ferrari's first F1 victory, and shown here circa 1952) famously said "back in my day, the drivers were fat and the tires were skinny."

Tech Speak

Road and Track

F1 is the technological pinnacle of motorsports and it has driven innovations we take for granted on the road cars of today. In fact some of the electronic systems that make our cars easier to drive have been banned from F1 on the grounds that they make the cars too quick or life too easy for the drivers: antilock brakes, traction control, and active suspension were all pioneered and perfected in F1.

This Ferrari Enzo engine bay shows how much has trickled down, or been inspired by, F1 technology. This V-12 was very much aped from an F1 design, and you'll note the inboard shocks and springs and intensive use of composites and lightweight metals.

Today's Inner Sanctums

A modern frontrunning F1 team employs over 1,000 people, a good many of whom never even attend races. Cost controls have caused headcounts to shrink and imposed caps on how many staff can travel to races, but F1 is still far from the days when one or two people designed the car and manufacture of the metal components would be outsourced before being assembled in-house. Now as much of the car as possible is built under one roof—in Ferrari's case, the engines as well as the cars. Enter the inner sanctum of the team HQ where the components are built and you'll find surprisingly few oily fingers. Hospital-like cleanliness rules: carbon-composite components are made by gluing layer upon layer of carbon-fiber sheets together in a mould that is then vacuum-sealed and baked in an oven-type device known as an autoclave. The number of sheets and the direction in which they're laid is carefully specified at the design stage. Specks of dust or air pockets between the layers can render a component useless. To exclude contaminants, key areas of the factory are only accessible by airlocked doors.

Nothing is left to chance in the build. Every component is quality tested and remains identifiable throughout its service life. Indeed, "lifing" is a little-known but crucial element of F1 operations. Because composite components weaken over time, every part has a given "life" beyond which it is liable to fail and so is replaced.

Research and development also demand the best equipment and highly qualified specialists. In the 2000s, when F1 was flush with tobacco-sponsorship money and car manufacturer largesse, and money was no object, leading teams viewed it as essential to have two or more wind tunnels, including at least one big enough to accommodate a full-scale car. Cost controls now restrict the teams to one tunnel and a maximum 60 percent scale model, with further limits on speeds the tunnel can simulate and how many "runs" can be performed. Increased computer processing power over the past decade has made

Ferrari is so large, and has been entrenched in F1 since the beginning of the modern era, it is one of those teams that can do nearly everything in house. While of course Scuderia Ferrari relies on various component suppliers, its design, aerodynamics, chassis and body building all take place in Maranello, and often share certain interfaces with the road car side of the house.

F1 Team HQs are tightly guarded locations and houses the team behind the team. Some build their own engines, most their own chassis, but no matter where things come from, they all come together here. Top teams also boast their own wind tunnels; this is Red Bull F1 Technology's Milton Keynes, England, facility.

The Mercedes F1 HQ and sports car
production facility in Woking, England,
is an modern, avant garde combination of
architecture, utility, and futurism. Note
the lake that's neatly incorporated into
the structure's design. Something like
1,000 designers, engineers, and other
racing and production staff occupy this
amazing property.

"virtual" research an important part of the mix, but it too is restricted by F1 rules and has some limits in scope. Certain elements of F1 car behavior—the turbulence induced by the front wheels, for instance—are impossible to simulate exactly.

To fast-track designs into the wind tunnel, teams use industrial-size rapid prototyping machines, in effect large-scale 3D printing. These work by firing lasers into a vat of a reactive substance (it can be a liquid or powder) that solidifies at the laser's focal point, creating an exact replica of the design in three dimensions. But with limited time permitted in the tunnel, it's never been more important to make the right choices at the design and conceptual stages.

Translating theoretical performance into reality is another key challenge. There's no guarantee the car will behave on-track as it did in the tunnel or in the computer. Teams often talk about "correlation," the extent to which real-life performance reflects R&D findings, or the more vague term "understanding the car," which essentially means they're sure the performance is there, they just haven't found the means of unlocking it yet.

Modern cost controls also mean drivers have fewer opportunities to test drive their cars in real conditions. Until the 2000s teams could test anywhere, any time, and would often rent out circuits to run alone, behind closed doors. Ferrari still has their own private test track, Fiorano, opposite the factory gates in Maranello, but regulations forbid them from running their current F1 cars there. Now there are generally just two preseason tests open to all, while individual teams are allowed a limited number of filming days.

As a result, F1 drivers now spend as much time hunkered down in an office with their engineers as they do on track during a grand prix weekend. *Drive to Survive* often gains access to such debriefs, but, in keeping with the show's amped-up dramatic remit, tech talk is usually left on the cutting room floor in favor of tense scenes when all isn't going well on track.

The strange looking series of rods, fixtures, and sensors affixed to this Red Bull machine gather primarily aerodynamic information from all of the car's surfaces possible, as every molecule of air that touches the car is in some way managed and optimized.

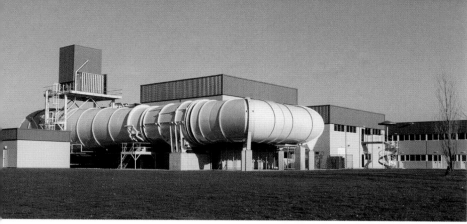

Early in an F1 machine's design career, aerodynamic testing is often accomplished using small-scale models with scaled-down wind tunnels. By the time a design is full grown, it's being tested in full-scale wind tunnels using 100 percent scale models and ultimately the real full-sized and fully equipped race car. This is a partial view of the tunnel at Williams F1's Oxfordshire England factory.

Aerodynamics: Flying on the Ground

Although some grand prix cars of the 1930s and 1950s had streamliner body shapes with partially enclosed wheels, aerodynamics remained poorly understood until the late 1970s, when teams began proper wind-tunnel research for the first time. Cars first sprouted wings, with the aim of creating downward pressure, in 1968. These primitive airfoils, usually mounted to the wheel hubs by tall, thin pillars, were rightly considered dangerous and quickly banned.

More structurally sound aerodynamic devices, including wings, were developed as engineers began to understand how airflow could be harnessed and F1 cars transitioned from tubular shapes to wedge profiles. The high-wing concept enjoyed a brief renaissance in 1997 when the Tyrrell team fitted elevated foils to the sides of their cars. These too were quickly banned, though it's believed because F1 ringmaster Bernie Ecclestone and FIA President Max Mosley thought they looked laughably ugly.

But what is the science behind F1 aerodynamic devices? An F1 car's front and rear wings work in the opposite way to those of a bird or an airplane, creating downward pressure rather than lift. Essentially this is suction: The wings are angled so that air passing underneath them is moving faster than the air flowing over them, producing a difference in pressure. The car is therefore sucked toward the ground by the lower air pressure beneath, enabling it to go around corners faster.

This is just one part of the wing's job. Every one of an F1 car's aerodynamic components has to work in harmony with those downstream of it—what aerodynamicists call the "flow structure." What this means in practice is the front wing has a huge influence on the overall aerodynamic efficiency of the car. As well as generating downforce, it steers air around the front wheels, minimizing the negative impact their wake turbulence has on the rest of the car. The front wing also maintains a smooth and consistent airflow under the car. In previous years the so-called diffuser, a sculpted underfloor tunnel between the rear wheels,

Wing design technology changes every year based on lessons learned, technological advancements, and rule changes. The earliest aero devices were single surface, or single element wings; and today five horizontal elements per side isn't unusual.

was a major contributor to downforce by accelerating airflow and creating lower pressure under the car.

The power of generating low-pressure areas beneath the car became an obsession for F1 designers in the late 1970s and the governing body struggled to contain it, wary of the safety implications of faster lap times.

Although eliminated in 1983 (by forcing all cars to be flat bottomed), "ground effect" made a comeback thirty-nine years later as F1 explored solutions to improve overtaking. To make trailing cars less sensitive to turbulence from cars ahead, the rules were changed to simplify the front and rear wings and render them less influential. As often

happens with big changes to the rule book, some teams adapted better than others.

Underfloor airflow is less sensitive to turbulence, making it easier for cars to run close to one another, so new formula for 2022 also dictated twin underbody tunnels that accelerate airflow and help generate negative pressure. Unfortunately a long-forgotten side effect of this philosophy reemerged: uncontrolled bouncing caused by the floor losing suction and springing up before being sucked back toward the ground. As with changes to the wings, some teams were worse affected than others, leading to more of the kind of behind-the-scenes rancor that adds to the *Drive to Survive* drama.

Cars began sporting all manner of wings and other aero devices in the 1960s. Wings are good and providing two things: increased cornering grip due to downforce and wind resistance or aerodynamic drag; the first is good, the latter not so much. Lotus mastermind Colin Chapman divined that airflow beneath the car could be used to help suck the car to the ground with less drag than ever more and ever larger wings; this "ground effect" principle was startling and proved without doubt on this Lotus 79 grand prix, which Mario Andretti drove to the 1978 world driving title.

Formula 1 Drive to Survive: The Unofficial Companion

We may not be able to see the particles that make up the air we breathe, but they're there. And when an F1 car moves through them, friction is the result. Aerodynamicists call it drag, and any surface of the car can contribute to it, although the wings are major contributors.

Drag influences speed and fuel efficiency so designers try to reduce it by any means possible. The cars are also equipped with a drag reduction system (DRS), introduced as an overtaking aid in 2011. On specific areas of the track (mostly straights), drivers can activate the DRS, which opens a flap on the rear wing.

DRS emerged from a device that was pioneered by McLaren in 2010 and quickly banned. They found that by channeling air through the car via a network of tubes and directing it over the suction surface of the rear wing, they could reduce downforce and drag, gaining 6 miles per hour or more in a straight line. The driver activated the system by pressing his knee against the tube where it passed through the cockpit. Not everything in F1 is as high tech as you might think.

That big open gap in this Mercedes-AMG rear wing is the DRS when activated; allowing less aero drag, and several miles per hour more top speed, depending on the track. Not everyone loves this technology, but it has made passing more prevelant, and likely safer, than in recent seasons before DRS was implemented.

F1 Engines: The Politics of Power

"He needs a driver *and* an engine." Cyril Abiteboul's snarky comment about Christian Horner (in Horner's presence) is a standout moment in *Drive to Survive* season 1. Having won four world championships together, Red Bull and Renault endured a messy divorce in 2018, during which Renault poached Red Bull driver Daniel Ricciardo and ceased supplying engines to Red Bull. Abiteboul thought he'd delivered the killing blow after years of rancour.

For much of the world championship's existence, building cars and making engines have been separate disciplines. Of the ten most successful teams in terms of race wins,

seven built just their cars and bought their engines from outside manufacturers. History is littered with failures brought on by teams trying to do everything under one roof and overstretching their resources. In the 1960s and 1970s the Ford-Cosworth V-8 democratized F1: It was powerful, affordable, and reliable. More significantly, Ford wasn't running a team, so they weren't competing against their own customers.

The competitive landscape has changed in recent years. The technology needed to build a racing engine is incredibly advanced, even more so in the hybrid era—

Several generations of Ferrari's seminal V-12 grand prix engines ruled Formula 1. As time and technology evolved, the old prancing war horse was rendered out of the business. Engine formulas changed seemingly at will, ranging from tiny, small displacement engines to large displacement torque monsters. Over time there have been four-cylinder F1 engines, V-6s, V-8s, V-10s, even V-16s, and then turbos and turbo/hybrids. Still the old-school, glorious-sounding V-12s out of Maranello remain huge in the record books and F1 fans' hearts.

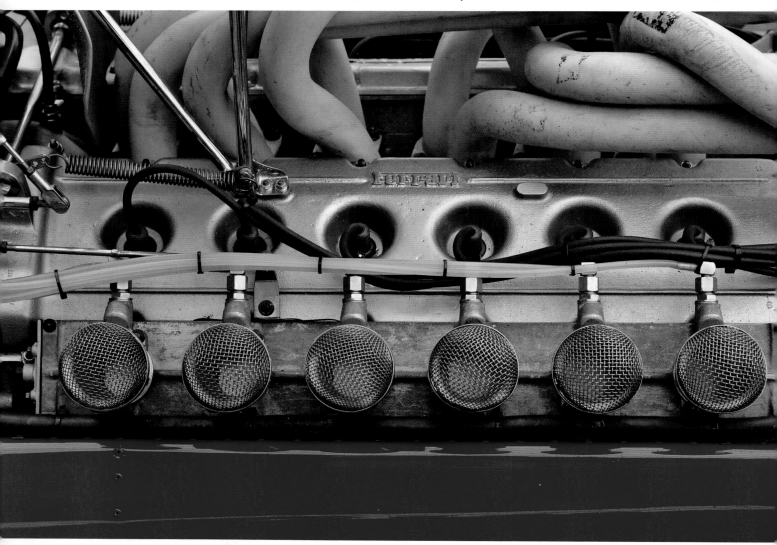

Cosworth's fabulous 3.0-liter DOHC V-8 somewhat democratized F1 engine selection beginning in the late 1960s. It was available in abundant supply and was relatively affordable, and Cosworth was not bound to supplying it or prevented from selling it to any particular team. Besides being super sturdy, its powerband was huge and broad. In naturally aspirated and later turbocharged forms, it served F1 (and USAC and CART Indy car racing) for decades, winning countless races and championships.

"HISTORY IS LITTERED WITH FAILURES BROUGHT ON BY TEAMS OVERSTRETCHING RESOURCES."

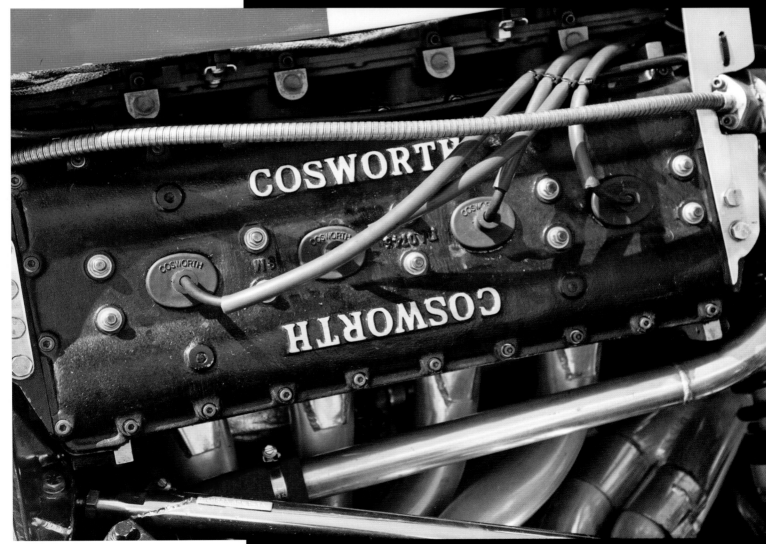

a rules package that was supposed to entice new entrants because it was more relevant to modern road cars. In reality there is only Mercedes, Ferrari, Renault, and Honda. Engine supply has taken on a political dimension. Mercedes was dominant in the early years of the hybrid era because they started earlier and nailed key technological problems first. Ferrari and Renault were caught short; Honda was initially way behind, having committed much later, only arriving in 2015.

It's supposed to be easy to chop and change between engine suppliers—the number and position of the mounting points that connect engine and chassis are written into the rules. But the fact is that if the car and engine designers are sitting around the same table at the conceptual stage, they can find better engineering compromises. The exception was the first couple of years of the hybrid era, when Mercedes was so far ahead that their customers were regularly beating the likes of Ferrari.

Red Bull was dissatisfied with the Renault hybrid engine's power and reliability. Renault's decision to return as a "works team" in 2016 provided the tipping point. The problem for Red Bull was that they were too good for Mercedes or Ferrari to want to supply them, which left just Honda.

It's a point glossed over in *Drive to Survive*, but the situation was less perilous for Red Bull than it appeared. Their "B-team," Toro Rosso, had been running Honda engines throughout 2018. So even as Abiteboul gloated, Horner knew Honda was coming good at last—and keen to work closely with one of the best teams in the business.

Honda has long been an F1 engine supplier; In fact, one time running a race-winning banshee screaming V-12 engine in its own team entry. This hybrid turbocharged V-6 dates to 2018.

Tech Speak

Fuel (If You Think It's Over)

At various points in history, F1 cars have run on some bizarre brews, including aviation fuel in the 1950s. While having supply arrangements with oil companies is commercially valuable for teams, having a fuel 'n' lubes partner can add up to a significant competitive advantage too—even though using a close relative of ordinary pump fuel has been mandatory since 1992. In 2022 F1 moved to E10, an 87-octane gas which is 10 percent ethanol.

For a publicity stunt in 2011, Ferrari compared its Shell V-Power race fuel with the equivalent pump product by running both in back-to-back tests in the same F1 car, with Fernando Alonso driving. He was only 9/10ths of a second slower with the pump fuel.

That's no surprise, given the tightness of the regulations. But to prevent cheating, the FIA regularly carries out spot tests during race weekends, checking that the fuel in the cars is an exact chemical match for the samples supplied in advance by the teams. It's very easy for fuel to become contaminated as it's transferred from one vessel to the other, so the suppliers of the leading teams—Shell, ExxonMobil, and Petronas—operate trackside labs to ensure their fuel is a match at all times. In addition, testing oil samples for contaminants, including microscopic metal shavings, can provide an early indicator of trouble. Since teams are now allowed only three engines and four gearboxes per driver per season, with strict penalties for going over those limits, a timely heads-up can prevent a damaging failure.

```
Over time, F1 engines have run on often
bizarre and highly volatile blends of
exotic fuels, gasolines, and additive—many
of which chemically resemble jet fuel.
Naturally every team guards and protects
its fuel stores, not only to prevent any
efforts to steal its secret blends, but to
avoid sabotage. Shell has been a long-time
stalwart fuel and lubricants provider to F1,
yet today several companies provide F1's
gas supply. A close relative to ordinary
pump gas has been mandated since 1992, and
as of 2002, F1 moved to E10, an 87 Octane
gas blended with 10 percent ethanol. F1 has
committed to introducing a 100% sustainable
bio fuel by 2026.
```

Inside an F1 Power Unit

In the hybrid era, engineers prefer to talk about "power units" rather than "engines" because of the sheer number of electrical systems that augment the turbocharged V-6 blocks. Adopting this formula required a huge cultural shift. Before 2014 F1 was *noisy*. It still is, but not to the same magnitude. As the 3-liter V-10s of the 1990s climbed through the rev range, they built to a powerful bellowing shriek. When 2.6-liter V-8s were brought in to try to control performance, engine manufacturers responded by finding more revs. In 2006 the Cosworth V-8 became the first racing engine to go past 20,000 rpm. To work in F1 at that time, or to be a fan, was to risk hearing loss if you didn't take precautions.

Today's 1.6-liter turbocharged hybrids are lower-revving and much easier on the ear, though the change proved controversial at the time. While the old guard still laments the passing of the V-10s and V-8s, F1 is now much more family friendly, as reflected by record-breaking ticket sales and TV audiences.

It's also leading the way in fuel efficiency. That may seem a peculiar goal, since motor racing historically involves burning lots of petrol, but a key element of the rules is that the cars can start the race with no more than 110 kilograms of fuel. Going fastest while using the least amount of fuel has driven incredible advances in technology. Burning petrol is an inherently inefficient process—the average road car engine converts only 20 percent or so of the fuel's potential energy into kinetic energy (i.e., driving the pistons up and down). F1 PUs currently achieve 52 percent by burning the fuel more efficiently and recycling the energy expelled from the exhaust, as well as by reclaiming energy from the brakes.

A Williams mechanic goes over the FW44 power unit at the 2022 Italian Grand Prix. While the old guard bemoans the passing of the V-10s and V-8s, today's turbocharged hybrids are easier on the environment and on the ear.

Internal Combustion Engine (ICE)

The most conventional element of the powertrain is the ICE, a 1-6-liter turbocharged V-6 with direct fuel injection, burning E10 petrol with a 10 percent ethanol component to lower CO_2 emissions.

Turbocharger

The turbo is essentially a pair of turbines connected by a shaft. The hot exhaust gases are directed through one of the turbines, causing it to spin. The turbine at the other end then compresses the air being drawn into the engine's combustion chambers, which can deliver a bigger bang. Since the exhaust gases are fundamentally wasted energy, this is part of the recycling process.

Motor Generator Unit–Heat (MGU-H)

This is the hybrid element most manufacturers struggled to get right. Part of the turbocharger assembly, it uses the movement of the turbine to generate electricity, which can be sent to the Energy Store or the MGU-K. It can also spin the turbines itself, eliminating "turbo lag," or the delay between the driver pressing the accelerator and the turbines spinning up to deliver their boost. This requires it to be capable of spinning at up to 100,000 rpm, a huge challenge for reliability.

Motor Generator Unit–Kinetic (MGU-K)

Connected to the rear wheels, this is a generator that reclaims kinetic energy from the movement of the rear wheels and can send it to the energy store. Mostly this happens during braking (or when drivers are told to "lift and coast" to save the brakes), which is why modern F1 cars feature "drive-by-wire" brakes on the rear wheels rather than a direct hydraulic connection to the pedal: the electronics modulate the pressure applied to the brake pads based on whether the MGU-K is reclaiming energy or not. Without this, the additional braking effect when the MGU-K kicks in might cause the rear wheels to lock up. The MGU-K can also direct energy back into the rear wheels to increase acceleration.

Nelson Piquet inspects the business end of his BMW turbocharged engine at the 1985 Portuguese Grand Prix.

Energy Store (ES)

While the rules allow for a variety of solutions, including supercapacitors and flywheels, for reliability and packaging reasons, all F1 engine manufacturers use conventional lithium-ion batteries to store the energy recovered via the hybrid systems. How much and when energy can be recovered or redeployed is governed by the rules. The energy store can harvest only 2 megajoules per lap from the MGU-K, but it can send four megajoules per lap to it (the equivalent of 161 horsepower). It can send unlimited amounts to and from the MGU-H. The restrictions on how much power can be sent to the rear wheels play a major role in a driver's attack or defense strategy. How much they use, and when, can be the difference between success and failure in an overtaking move or frustrating another driver's attempt to pass.

VELAS

#essenceFerrari

A view of the Ferrari's rear brakes taken at the 2022 British Grand Prix. Connected to the rear wheels, the MGU-K reclaims kinetic energy from the movement of the rear wheels and can also direct energy back to the rear wheels to increase acceleration.

MGU-H

This diagram of the Ferrari 059/3 power unit calls out the MGU-H (motor generator unit-heat), which uses the turbine's movement to generate electricity.

Chapter 4

BUILD IT AND THEY WILL COME

F1 CIRCUITS

One large part of the appeal of *Drive to Survive* is F1's traveling circus. During the course of a race season, Formula 1 visits five continents. F1's tracks—or "circuits"—are the stages on which this grand circus performs. But whether purpose built or laid out on city streets, not all circuits are created equal—and with cars capable of hitting speeds over 200 miles per hour, there's a lot of work to do to keep everyone safe.

"Build it and They Will Come," indeed. Bahrain International Circuit was a complicated design and undertaking, owing largely to the hot desert landscape. Here Tsunoda Yuki and his Scuderia AlphaTauri AT03 see action during the 2022 Gulf Air Bahrain Grand Prix.

Location, Location, Location

Race drivers once had to be vigilant for all kinds of unexpected obstacles. Telegraph poles, houses, walls, ditches, tramlines, spectators, stray dogs, cars coming the other way—all were potential hazards in grand prix racing's wilder days when events were usually held on closed-off sections of public highway.

Grands prix at permanent (or semi-permanent) facilities now make up most of the season. Purpose-built tracks have a consistency of surface and infrastructure, the spectators get a good view (mostly) from a safe distance, and there's enough space for cars to run offtrack without immediately

hitting a barrier. The downside is that most circuits are at out-of-town locations, which are hard to reach if you don't have a car, so they're not an easy or inexpensive entry point for new fans—which, as viewers of *DTS* know, doesn't mean the bleachers sit empty.

Street circuits such as Monaco, Azerbaijan, Singapore, and Las Vegas are often more hazardous because of the tight confines of the urban landscape and the proximity of the barriers. But their locations can attract more local people who might otherwise be inclined to make the journey.

The street circuit dedicated to the running of the Monaco Grand Prix is one of the most attractive and certainly most romantic on the F1 calendar. Even though it's evolved considerably since its beginnings, primarily in terms of safety barriers, reconfigured corners, and lighting inside its iconic tunnel, it's still a tricky drive—particularly given the speed of today's cars. Were it presented today to Formula 1 management and drivers, it's doubtful it would be approved or accepted as an official race venue. The drivers who have mastered it, such multitime winners Graham Hill and the incomparable Ayrton Senna, are hailed as GOATs for their success here. This marvelous shot comes from the opening lap of the 1977 race.

Unprecedented obstacles are everywhere you look at Monaco. In spite of some widening over the years and other additional safety measures, there's lots to hit in the form of safety railing, buildings, safety vehicles on course, and such. It's gorgeous to be sure, but very tricky to drive well and fast, and even tougher on which to pass.

Build It and They Will Come: F1 Circuits

Originally a long, bumpy, and very fast constant radius bend that carried drivers through a full 180 degrees, the Peraltada gained notoriety during a non-championship test event before Mexico joined the F1 calendar. Local hero Ricardo Rodríguez lost control of his Lotus there when its suspension failed, with fatal consequences. The corner remained a signature feature of the circuit despite several high-profile incidents: Ayrton Senna rolled his McLaren there during practice for the 1991 Mexican GP. That race also featured one of the most spectacular overtakes of all time, when Nigel Mansell went around the outside of Gerhard Berger at the Peraltada—a feat of supreme bravery at racing speeds. Unfortunately the run-off area was too small for modern cars and nonextendable, so on the current layout, the track dodges inside the Foro Sol baseball stadium, which was built just within the curve of the corner while the GP was on hiatus between 1992 and 2015.

"

AYRTON SENNA ROLLED HIS MCLAREN THERE DURING PRACTICE FOR THE 1991 MEXICAN GP."

The home of the Mexican Grand Prix is a fast, challenging course. It's also brilliantly colorful, as are the enthusiastic attendees, particularly when there's a Mexican or Latin driver in the field or on the winner's podium.

Designing and Building a Circuit

Whatever the environment, a huge amount of science and technical requirements go into designing and building a circuit. To meet FIA Grade One requirements—that is, for the track to be able to host a grand prix—permanent circuits must have a minimum track width of 12 meters, straights can't be longer than 2 kilometers, the grid spots have to be 8 meters apart, and the pitlane entry has to be 12 meters. The circuit needs to have a permanent medical center too. You'll often hear drivers complain over the radio to their race engineer about circuits being bumpy, but this is relative: FIA Grade One status allows for surface variations to be no greater than 0.08 inch up or down over the course of 13 feet.

Spa Francorchamp is a famous and historic circuit; Known for dizzying top speeds and dramatic elevation changes, it's beautiful to watch and a thrill a minute to drive.

The famous Hungaroring is huge and known for its long, sweeping, semicircular corners. It's surrounded primarily by rural farmland.

Once considered among F1's most challenging corners (and now derided by keyboard warriors for being "too easy"), this section will make you wince when you watch the onboard footage of the Racing Point drivers banging wheels here in *Drive to Survive* S1:E6. The original public road plunged downward, then took a sharp left-right as it hit the bottom of the valley and crossed the river that gives the corner its name (owing to the mineral content the water has a reddish tint). There's then a sharp uphill ramp and a left corner over a blind crest—that's Raidillon, where Formula 2 driver Anthoine Hubert lost his life in 2019 (*DTS* S2:E6). On the other side of the tire barrier, there's a steep, wooded drop to the valley floor, which required large-scale excavation to extend the runoff area.

Eau Rouge is a fast uphill right hander that never fails to figure in F1 racing history in terms of significant passes, accidents, or other impactful moments. It's also a beautiful and historic course, surrounded by deep green forest.

Formula 1 Drive to Survive: The Unofficial Companion

Alongside Eau Rouge, this fast left-hander remains one of F1's signature tests of bravery despite adjustments to make it safer. Modern F1 cars have sufficient grip and aerodynamic downforce to carry huge speeds through here, but it was once the case that when something went wrong here, it went very wrong—once the car started getting away from the driver, there was no way of getting it back. Toyota's Allan McNish provided a case study in this during qualifying for the 2002 Japanese GP: His car slid onto the curb at the exit, the back end more than the front, and instinctively McNish tried to correct the slide by steering into it. The result was the rear end gripped up again and then slid the other way, sending him into the barrier backward with an impact speed of 175 miles per hour and 69 G. He ended up on the other side with his car shorn in two.

Alan McNish's trajectory toward (and through) the barrier at the exit of 130R at the 2002 Japanese Grand Prix is written in black lines on the asphalt.

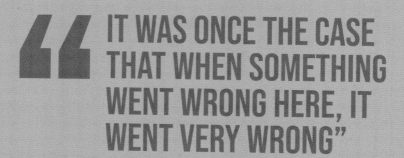

"IT WAS ONCE THE CASE THAT WHEN SOMETHING WENT WRONG HERE, IT WENT VERY WRONG"

Track designers map out layouts down to a matter of inches and simulate them carefully to work out what the speeds might be and where the barriers need to go. The layout of the Miami Grand Prix circuit around the Hard Rock Stadium went through thirty-six permutations before all the stakeholders settled on a final design. One of the final changes involved relocating the entire pitlane and pit complex to the outside rather than the inside of the track, because Miami Dolphins owner Stephen Ross wanted to be able to use the pit buildings for other purposes for the rest of the year.

An incredible amount of thought then goes into the details. How much runoff area is required? How will the spectators get in and out? Where do the barriers go? What type of barriers will they be? Where will the marshal stations and access points go? Simulations help to predict the drivers' sightlines, which dictate the locations of the marshal posts and signal boards. They also help predict potential danger areas where cars may crash; here they need a means of extracting those cars quickly.

Speed calculations inform the types of barriers used at different points of a circuit. Armco is designed to deform progressively so impact is dissipated along the length of the metal panels rather than concentrated in a single area. But Armco is not appropriate for all situations and is used only in areas deemed to be low risk. That doesn't mean they won't take a hit (see Romain Grosjean's accident in *DTS* S3:E9 "Man on Fire"). Barriers, made from multiple stacks of road tires held together by rubber belts, can manage impact forces better, but there's a risk of the car penetrating the barrier, making it difficult to get the driver out. Tecpro is the favored solution for high-risk, high-speed areas: It's a system of interconnected hollow polyethylene blocks, faster to install and quicker to repair than a tire barrier.

There's also catch fencing to consider. It has to offer high levels of protection while enabling trackside staff and spectators to see through. After a series of accidents in U.S. IndyCar racing, the FIA began to lay down specific standards for what impact forces the catch fencing has to be capable of managing: the test involves firing an actual car at the fencing at 75 miles per hour with an impact angle of 20 degrees. To pass the test, the fence cannot deflect or move more than 3 meters from the installation site.

This is the fiery aftermath of Haas driver Romain Grosjean's crash just at the start of the 2020 Baharin Grand Prix. In spite of the horrific images initially captured on the television coverage, Grosjean's injuries were confined to second-degree burns on his hands. He retired from F1, and has since joined the IndyCar series in North America. Of course, the doctor-equipped Mercedes F1 safety car was on scene immediately to see to the driver's well being.

Sprightly and energetic even into his eighties, Sir Jackie Stewart crops up regularly in the background of *Drive to Survive* episodes: He's the guy in the tartan. He nearly didn't make it this far.

Spa-Francorchamps was longer in Stewart's race days (8.76 miles) and still made from public roads. The race in question started in dry weather, but on lap one the heavens opened. Seven drivers spun out, including Stewart, whose car aquaplaned at 170 miles per hour into a telegraph pole—then a roadside cottage, then a farm building. American driver Bob Bondurant had to borrow a wrench from a spectator to remove Stewart's steering wheel so he could be pried out of the mangled cockpit. In the 25 minutes it took to get Stewart out of the car, no marshals arrived to help. By then, he was soaked in fuel and suffering chemical burns on top of his other injuries. When he regained consciousness in the building that served as the medical center, he was on a stretcher on the floor with the dirt and cigarette butts. The only doctor present was a gynecologist. Stewart was packed into an ambulance for a hospital in Liege, but the ambulance driver got lost.

Unsurprisingly Stewart made it his mission to execute change. What's remarkable is the opposition he faced from entrenched interests: Promoters who didn't want to invest in better facilities and even some drivers who thought he was being a wimp. But Stewart galvanized the drivers to push for proper medical facilities, more and better-trained marshals, stronger barriers, and safer circuits. They even boycotted Spa and Germany's Nürburgring, much to the chagrin of some—but they prevailed in the end.

A young John Young Stewart (before he was Sir Jackie) was an early, vocal, and influential champion of improving racing safety. He pushed for the reconfiguration of dangerous race conditions, the use of full-faced helmets, and the need for ever better trackside medical personnel, equipment, and facilities. He also was a successful driver with his twenty-seven Grands Prix victories and three world driving titles.

The "Wee Scot" is one cool dude, today as in the 1960s. The now Sir Jackie Stewart's trademark longish hair and tartan plaid clothing accessories created a look forever tied to him, and the now octogenarian remains a common sight at nearly every F1 race. He's often consulted and deeply regarded for his authoritative experience and viewpoints.

This first lap melee was tragic in many ways. The pileup and fire cost Lotus driver Ronnie Peterson his life; his Lotus teammate, Mario Andretti, won the championship on this day, but lost one of his best friends, ending any notion of celebration. If there was any positive force that day, this avoidable accident helped bring about a revised lap 1, a green flag, and starting procedures aimed at minimizing the accordion effect that caused this awful wreck, injuries, and loss of life.

Accidents That Changed F1

Ronnie Peterson, Monza, 1978

The first corner at Monza has always been a flash point, especially on the first lap. In 1978 the field was signaled to go before the final cars had come to a halt on the grid, sparking a multicar shunt at turn one for which Riccardo Patrese was unfairly blamed (and banned). Lotus driver Ronnie Peterson, running second in the drivers' championship, suffered multiple leg fractures but wasn't considered at risk. He later died in the hospital after suffering kidney failure brought on by blood poisoning.

It was clear that starting procedures needed tighter control. But the most immediate consequence was the hiring of Professor Sid Watkins as F1's permanent medical delegate, with a remit that included following the field at the start in a medical car so he could quickly reach the scene of any first-lap accident.

The first-responder role today is occupied by Dr. Ian Roberts, who is also on permanent standby throughout races and

is automatically called when car sensors register a high impact (the drivers also carry accelerometers in their ears). The medical car is a high-performance vehicle—currently rotating between Mercedes and Aston Martin—that carries everything required to stabilize a driver's condition trackside before they're taken to the medical center. To ensure it arrives quickly, it's driven by 2003 British Formula 3 Champion Alan van der Merwe. In the *Drive to Survive* episode "Man on Fire," the producers employ liberal use of multiple angles and slow motion to depict Romain Grosjean's accident in the 2020 Bahrain Grand Prix, such that you might think it took minutes for help to arrive. In fact, the medical car arrived within 10 seconds.

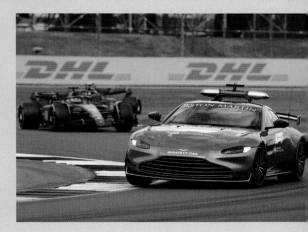

Aston Martin is the current co-sponsor/ provider of F1's Safety and Medical cars; this Medical Car is A-M's über sport and high-performance "Shooting Brake" or sport/ utility vehicle called the DBX.

Legendary Circuits: What Makes a Great F1 Venue?

While the likes of Silverstone in England and Spa-Francorchamps in Belgium get grand introductions in *Drive to Survive* sweeping drone shots, soaring music, evocative scene-setting by drivers and the talking heads—other circuits slide into view with just a screen caption. Just as *DTS* seems to favor certain circuits, some venues are beloved by drivers and F1 personnel while others are considered a chore, either because their layouts are bland and unchallenging or getting there is a logistical nightmare.

What characterizes a "drivers' circuit"? Typically they've developed almost organically, based around roads or local topographical features that were already there. Silverstone's layout has evolved, but it still mostly follows the line of the perimeter roads from its previous life as an airfield. Drivers love the high speeds and the flowing nature of the corners, particularly the Maggotts-Becketts-Chapel switchbacks (a feature borrowed by the Circuit of the Americas in Texas, also a favored venue). Spa is now a permanent circuit, but it was once a connected series of public roads that rose and plunged through the Ardennes hills, dodging past rivers and forests.

Suzuka in Japan was built as a test track for Honda, so it aimed to pack as many different corner types as possible into a tight piece of real estate—on a hillside. Hence its unique figure-eight layout and corners that really test chassis dynamics and driver finesse. And while Monza's chicanes are a necessary blight (for safety reasons), the sheer speeds and the passion of the crowd make the Italian track a driver favorite. As for Monaco, it may be impossible to overtake on the tight street circuit, but the skill required to skim the barriers at high speed without hitting them for lap after lap make it tough but satisfying.

Conversely many clean-sheet designs have lacked a certain magic no matter how much time and money has been thrown at them. For all the spectacle—the day-into-night format, the midrace light show, and the postrace firework display—the Abu Dhabi Grand Prix is generally disliked owing to the layout of the Yas Marina circuit, which manages to be too striving and too boring at the same time. A redesign ahead of the 2021 race did little to improve it. A frequent criticism of this and other tracks designed by Hermann Tilke is an overreliance on slow corners with off-camber sloping surfaces, placed there to encourage drivers to make mistakes. But F1 drivers don't make many mistakes.

Another circuit F1, generally speaking, will be pleased never to visit again is the Sochi Autodrom in Russia. A low-grip surface,

a layout dictated by existing buildings (the 2014 Winter Olympics venue), and the generally hateful process of actually getting there (unless you were on a private jet) made this one to miss.

The F1 circuit in Sochi, Russia, is a central part of the sports complex built for the Sochi Olympics. As of this writing, the Russian Grand Prix is currently suspended from the F1 calender stemming from Russia's war against Ukraine.

Jules Bianchi's ultimately fatal crash raised difficult questions—along with answers many didn't want to hear.

Rain late in an already delayed Japanese Grand Prix brought slippery conditions and greatly reduced visibility. On lap forty-three Bianchi lost control of his car at the Dunlop corner and hit an extraction vehicle that was attending to another car that had spun out. Some of the preimpact footage is shown in the *DTS* season 1 episode "The Next Generation," which follows Charles Leclerc, Bianchi's friend and godson. Bianchi's head hit the extraction vehicle, leaving him in a vegetative state until his eventual death.

So many questions. Why stick to a 3 p.m. start time in Japan in October, when poor weather and low light were likely? Why was the safety car not deployed while the other car was being retrieved? Why did it take so long for the FIA to understand the severity of the accident? Why was Bianchi driven to the hospital rather than flown by helicopter?

What emerged from the official inquiry was that Bianchi didn't slow down enough for the yellow flags signaling the first accident and that he tried to deploy a failsafe system that cuts the engine when the driver presses the brake and throttle at the same time. This didn't work because his car's brake-by-wire system wasn't compatible. The medical helicopter was unavailable because of low cloud cover.

So many of the GP races run at Suzuka have been in the wet, some of which caused tragic wrecks, loss of life, and altered championship scenarios. Jules Bianchi's ultimately fatal crash raised difficult questions—along with answers many didn't want to hear.

The result was a tightening of procedures around yellow flags and the development of the virtual safety car system, which is now used to slow down all cars by a specified amount almost instantly. Track drainage was also improved, new rules governed how long races could be delayed, and sessions are now stopped if the medical helicopter can't take off. The colored light panels around the track that relay the flag status have been improved (although their visibility is still sometimes open to question—Lewis Hamilton failing to see one earned a penalty and opened the door for Pierre Gasly to win the 2020 Italian Grand Prix covered in *DTS* S3:E6).

And while the inquiry found that no impact structure could have survived the crash, Bianchi's accident added momentum to the development of the halo cockpit protection system introduced in 2017.

The Virtual Safety Car system was one of a number of changes introduced after Jules Bianchi's accident at Suzuka. The electronic display boards were also upgraded to improve visibility.

Dead on the Road: When Circuits Die

If you visit France's champagne region, be sure to take in one of the area's less heralded tourist attractions. West of the city, on the D27 road leading to the village of Gueux, you'll find a remarkable sight: a grandstand, pit complex, and signaling tower largely restored to period accuracy by local enthusiasts. This is (almost) all that remains of the Reims-Gueux circuit, former home of the French Grand Prix and the site of Mercedes' first world championship victory.

You'll have to use a little imagination as you head around the lap. A roundabout now stands at the beginning of what was once a dangerously fast corner. The great Juan Manuel Fangio said he would glance over at the cornfield to his right to judge the speed and direction of the wind before he committed to going flat out.

Vanishingly few former grand prix venues are treated with such reverence. Go 125 miles north and you'll find an area of Belgium famous for being the site of the Battle of Waterloo. Not far from there, an industrial estate is growing up where once stood the unloved Nivelles-Baulers circuit, site of two Belgian Grands Prix in the 1970s when Spa-Francorchamps was considered too dangerous to race on.

While some venues, such as Brands Hatch in England, fell off the calendar because F1 cars became too fast for them, most of these remained in business serving other race series. New-build tracks have fared less well, battered by the twin forces of politics and commerce. This is a consequence of the way the commercial winds have been blowing over the past decades. The leveraged acquisition of F1's commercial rights by various entities over the years has created debts to service, and race promoters have felt the squeeze, often crowded out by government-funded races in nations eager to put themselves on the map. There was a time when Silverstone's place was under constant threat and even Spa is to become an irregular regular, rotating in and out of the calendar to make way for other races. Nivelles-Baulers' promoter went bust and couldn't even afford to complete the originally planned circuit layout. Having alternated between the road-based courses of Reims and Rouen until the early 1960s, the French Grand Prix went on a tour of the country via several new-builds dictated by regional politics, including a vanity project

A shame and a waste turns out to be the current state of affairs at the Buddh International Circuit, which hosted F1 races between 2011 and 2013. Unfortunately money issues and politics currently see it off the F1 calendar, unfortunate as it's a well-designed and up-to-date facility that the drivers seemed to enjoy racing on.

The historic Reims-Gueux circuit hasn't been used for Formula 1 or professional sports car racing since the 1960s, but its original pit structures and main grandstand still exist and the portion of track that was the main front straight is open and accessible to the public at no cost. The structures definitely wear their years and patina, but the paintwork, logos, and graphics were all faithfully restored and look fresh and colorful. It's worth a trip to this wonderful monument to racing history if you're heading to or from Le Mans.

LA COMMUNE DE GUEUX
ET LES
AMIS DU CIRCUIT DE GUEUX

vous souhaitent
la bienvenue

DUNLOP

paid for by pastis magnate Paul Ricard (who named the track after himself) and Dijon-Prenois, championed by multisportsman and local hero Francois Chambelland. It finally ended up at Magny-Cours in central France, not because that circuit had any special merit but because it was located in the home province of the country's then president.

The attrition rate has been particularly high among modern tracks built with the sole purpose of bringing F1 to a particular country. It's said that Bernie Ecclestone, F1's former commercial boss, had a lightbulb moment in the 1980s when he did the deal to add the Australian Grand Prix to the calendar. After years of dealing with local promoters who were unreliable and prone to inconvenient bankruptcies, Ecclestone loved it when a representative of the South Australian government flew to London to hand over the check in person. But Sepang in Malaysia provided the template for what might be called the big-bucks national prestige project: government-subsidized new-build tracks with fancy architecture that look great on TV.

Sepang lasted from 1999 until 2017. The official reason given for dropping out of F1 was the rising cost of hosting the race and declining ticket sales. It never attracted a large crowd because the tickets were too expensive for locals. Rather the political will to underwrite the ongoing expense ran out: the cost outweighed the benefits.

At least Sepang is still used. Other tracks funded by local government largesse in Korea and India hosted just a handful events before falling victim to regime change in local politics. They now lie almost dormant, used only for small-scale events such as track days.

Sepang was a visually and architecturally interesting facility, particularly due to its shell-shaped grandstand shades, beneficial during bright hot days or cold wet rainy race dates.

Formula 1 Drive to Survive: The Unofficial Companion

Formula 1 Drive to Survive: The Unofficial Companion

So tight that modern F1 cars are specially adapted to steer around it, this hairpin corner has had many names through the years, and not just because the hotel that stands over the site has changed hands so many times. It used to be Monaco's railway station, and the drivers of passing trains would often make unplanned halts on the bridge during the race to give passengers a view of the action. Since Monaco is a tiny piece of real estate, very little has changed in terms of the flow of the road in this section since the Principality hosted its first Grand Prix in 1929. It's a continuous slope down, even through the corner, so for a fraction of a second the cars are steering with just one wheel touching the track surface.

This ultra wide-angle fisheye shot of Monaco's famous hairpin shows more of the complexity, color, and romance of the principality's historic Grand Prix. The cars barrel down the hill prior to the turn-in point and still carry considerable speed through the corner. Over time many drivers have attempted a late-braking pass just prior to entering the turn—sometimes they get away with it, sometimes not so much.

Put simply, there's no better place in the world to watch how fast an F1 car can travel through a flowing set of corners when it's loaded up on downforce and grippy tires. This is a make-or-break section in terms of lap time, so in qualifying the drivers will be fully committed. It's the speed of the direction changes that blow the mind, even though modern F1 cars are so much heavier than their predecessors.

"

THERE'S NO BETTER PLACE IN THE WORLD TO WATCH HOW FAST AN F1 CAR CAN TRAVEL"

Silverstone is one of Formula 1's most storied venues; it's large, sprawling, surrounded by the New Forest, and blisteringly fast.

Formula 1 Drive to Survive: The Unofficial Companion

It's been reconfigured time and time again for safety reasons, but the section of track that swoops around Monaco's harbor-front swimming pool remains one of the toughest sections of what is already F1's most difficult circuit. The barriers are a driver's constant companion around a lap of this narrow circuit, but the direction changes required here demand utter precision. It is a question of millimeters.

Italian driver Alex Caffi gave a graphic demonstration of what can go wrong here when his Footwork-Porsche slid wide into the barriers during practice for the 1991 race. The TV crew weren't paying attention (as a backmarker, Caffi was of little interest), so the only extant footage is low-res black-and-white video from a trackside security camera. Caffi came to rest sitting in the only unbroken section of the car, with the engine still attached.

This section is much safer now, but it is still challenging. The main pinch point is the final right-left as the drivers pass the pool: It's very easy to clip the barrier on the inside of the right-hander and crack a wheel or break the suspension. That's what caused Max Verstappen to miss qualifying in 2018 and Charles Leclerc to not take up his pole position in 2021 (*DTS* S4:E3).

Why doesn't every F1 venue have an Olympic swimming pool inside of the track surface? Because they're not Monaco, that's why. Note the parking lot traffic jam of gazillion-dollar yachts and expensive apartments and blue water just beyond. The passages of track and corners that swoop by this sparkling blue pool complex are fast and more than a little treacherous.

Chapter 5

HOUSE RULES

GOVERNING F1

Formula 1 rules are necessarily complex and sometimes arcane: With high-performance cars circulating racetracks at speed, there's safety to consider and fairness to be maintained. There's also the matter of ten highly motivated teams staffed by clever and innovative engineers, all determined to bend—if not break—those regulations. In fact, given the high stakes, F1's governing body, Fédération Internationale de l'Automobile (FIA), sees fit to maintain *two* rule books for the series.

Lewis Hamilton leads the Red Bulls at the 2021 Abu Dhabi Grand Prix—a race that would end in no small amount of controversy and dash Hamilton's hopes for an eighth drivers' title.

Two Books to Rule Them All

F1 technical regulations run to 158 pages, prescribing car dimensions, weights, permissible curvatures and straight lines, essential equipment, locations of certain elements, and the forces various areas of the cars must be able to withstand when tested. There are precise definitions and measurements and there are gnomic, open-ended generalizations: e.g. "Dangerous construction: the stewards may exclude any vehicle whose construction is deemed to be dangerous."

The ever-growing sporting regulations run to 117 pages as of late 2022. This is the document team managers must carry in their heads. It covers everything from general terms and conditions (which now include the proviso that teams must hold FIA environmental accreditation) to the operating procedures of events, how protests and appeals may be lodged, how on-track incidents are dealt with, and the length of races. It also covers a driver's duties, from what license they must hold to when they need to show up for the national anthem, what they're expected to do during a race, and where they have to go afterward.

Both sets of regulations are subject to change during the season, and many elements have evolved over time. Take for example the simple-sounding stipulation introduced in 1994: "The driver must drive alone and unaided at all times." This accompanied the ban on driver-assistance systems such as antilock brakes, traction and launch control, and active suspension. In recent years, it was the given rationale for a short-lived crackdown on drivers being coached over the radio by their engineers.

F1 regulations also must evolve to face the challenges posed by attempts to bend or circumvent them. These rules are specific in places where those challenges are known, open-ended in areas that might need rapid reaction. It's rare that a year goes by without the FIA publishing at least one "technical directive" clarifying or revising existing rules.

The FIA is also responsible for overseeing the smooth running of race events. That's why it employs a consistent set of officials such as technical delegate Jo Bauer; single-seater technical director Nikolas Tombazis was a senior aerodynamicist at Benetton, McLaren, and Ferrari. The race director role is currently occupied by Niels Wittich after the removal of Michael Masi in the wake of the 2021 Abu Dhabi Grand Prix furore (*DTS* S4:E10).

The FIA often holds press conference–style meetings to announce and discuss rules and technical mandate changes and updates. From left, über-successful racing car designer, builder, and engineer Ross Brawn; Nikolas Tombazis, FIA head of single-seater technical matters; and Chase Carey, Formula 1 group chairman.

Ross Brawn

Nikolas Tombazis

Chase Carey

FORMULA 1 EMIRATES UNITED STATES GRAND PRIX

F1 2019

Ranged against these officials is a veritable army of the cleverest engineers on the planet. They can and will test the rules to the limit. Some senior engineers, such as Red Bull's Adrian Newey, often complain that F1's rules stifle innovation. This is nothing new—such gripes have always dogged officials. There is an irony here: The very reason F1's rules have succumbed to bloat is that these geniuses are constantly at work to flout them.

Finally it's obvious that behind these rules is the imperative of safety. For example, the deaths of Roland Ratzenberger and Ayrton Senna during the 1994 San Marino Grand Prix weekend, along with several other serious accidents that weekend and subsequently, prompted widespread rules changes in the following months. The technical regulations were amended to slow the cars down and, over the years to come, they encompassed more strict crash-testing measures.

A pitlane speed limit was introduced with a clearly defined beginning and end. Up until this point, drivers could and did go as fast as they dared.

Another consequence was the standardization of the safety car and the (mostly) clearly defined set of regulations governing its use. At Imola, the safety car, though it had a professional at the wheel (F3 racer Max Angelelli), was an ordinary road model. It's now a modified high-performance car—and F1 drivers still complain about it being too slow.

The FIA is an ever-present source in the administration of F1 activities, rules-making, and rules enforcement. This massive truck is at every F1 race, housing the leadership, staff, and engineers intended and needed to keep the game on the up and up—to the extent possible.

Two important members of the Red Bull F1 braintrust: team principal Christian Horner (left) and chief technical officer and race car designer extraordinare Adrian Newey (right). Newey has enjoyed a distinguished design career, particularly in F1, having conceived and penned many race and championship winners.

Gordon Murray (left) stands about 6-foot-4, while former Brabham team owner Bernie Ecclestone is perhaps a foot shorter, yet both are big guys in the Formula 1-O-Sphere. Murray is among the best and most successful engineers and car designers ever, while Ecclestone served many years as "F1 czar," deserving much of the credit for making F1 the multibillion-dollar international sport and marketing machine that it is today.

At Brabham in the 1970s and '80s, South African–born Gordon Murray designed some astoundingly quick and innovative race cars—as well as a couple that tested the limits of the rules.

With the Brabham BT46B "fan car," a rear-mounted fan in effect sucked the car closer to the ground, increasing grip (the mechanical layout of the Alfa Romeo flat-twelve engine prevented him from copying the underfloor aerodynamics of rivals). Perhaps even more cleverly, he designed it in such a way that he could prove to officials that the fan served an engine-cooling function, thereby circumventing the ban on movable aerodynamic devices.

Later, with the Cosworth V-8-powered BT49C, Murray developed an ingenious workaround for rules that insisted on a minimum ride height for the car. The clearance was tested by using a wooden block that officials slid under the car: Murray built the BT49C's bodywork on a pneumatic strut that kept the outer shell at legal height when the car was at rest. On track the aerodynamic forces pushed the bodywork down, enabling the ground-effect channels within to work at maximum effect.

It'll surprise nobody that Gordon Murray's Brabham "fan car" was immediately controversial. Having won its first race it was withdrawn, much to Murray's chagrin, in the face of protests from rival teams.

The "Bridge of Doom"

Every race weekend, the cars are checked for compliance with the rules at the FIA weighbridge, known informally among the teams as "the bridge of doom." The process is more officially known as scrutineering: the teams are responsible for proving their cars' legality to a panel of experienced judges led by the FIA's Jo Bauer.

Some tests are simpler than others. Dimensional requirements of various parts, including the width and height of the car, are proved (or otherwise) by whether they fit in a box. Other tests are more precise, such as those aimed at curbing flexible aerodynamic devices: specific loads are applied to areas of the floor and the front and rear wings to make sure they don't deflect beyond a permitted tolerance (in 2021 the FIA also made teams add graphics to their wings, which are continuously monitored on track via high-speed cameras).

Since this is a sport where performance is dictated by marginal gains, the difference between legality and illegality is often marginal. During the 2021 Brazilian Grand Prix weekend, Lewis Hamilton's qualifying time was canceled when the gap between his rear-wing elements was found to be 0.2 millimeters too large on one side when the DRS was open. The team said two screws had fallen out.

Sometimes, the teams themselves take an active role in flushing out cheats, if in a backhanded (some might say underhanded) manner. It's established precedent that teams run certain innovations by the FIA technical director to parse their legality. Teams also use this procedure to frustrate rivals they suspect of cheating because the FIA notifies all teams of its decision via a "technical directive."

For instance, Team A might suspect Team B is cheating by fitting a sprung device to the front of their car's floor. This device provides enough resistance to enable the floor to pass the FIA's deflection test, but then deflects under the greater aerodynamic loads the car encounters while on track, enabling the floor to deflect too. So Team A writes to the FIA, mentioning no names, but saying they're considering fitting such a system to their car. Helpfully, they also include a technical diagram illustrating how it might be done. The FIA responds by writing to all the teams saying that no such system is permissible, and it will be tightening the testing procedures to suit.

Sound far-fetched? It's what McLaren did to Ferrari at the beginning of the 2007 season.

F1 scrutineering (a.k.a. tech inspection) is serious stuff, carried out using lots of sophisticated measuring equipment. The scrutineers may ask a team to tear the car down to the smallest bits to ensure everything deep inside these sophisticated machines is to spec—or not.

The genius driver, Mario Andretti (left) and the genius engineer and car builder, Lotus doyen Colin Chapman, conspired to earn the World Driving Championship in 1978 with the advanced Lotus 79 Cosworth, which began setting the tone for the future development of "ground effects" as a means of vehicular downforce with minimal drag. Andretti had a rocky year with Lotus in 1977, and despite Enzo Ferrari dangling an offer to drive for the Scuderia in front of him, elected to stick with Lotus and the promise of the new car. Good move, as it turned out to be his magic carpet in F1.

 CHAPMAN EMPLOYED SOME OF THE MOST TALENTED ENGINEERS IN MOTOR RACING."

F1 champion (and future Indy 500 winner) Jim Clark pilots the cigar-like Lotus 25, a legendarily light F1 machine, at the 1964 Monaco Grand Prix.

Colin Chapman was what you might euphemistically call "an operator." The Lotus team founder established his business under a railway arch in North London in the 1950s and quickly gained a reputation as an innovator. He was also someone with whom, after shaking hands, you might take the precaution of checking your watch was still attached.

A creator in his own right, Chapman employed some of the most talented engineers in motor racing. His cars were fast, usually fragile, almost always cutting edge. In the 1960s the Lotus 25 led the way in monocoque construction (see chapter 2). Imagine the ire of his customers who had bought spaceframe-chassis Lotus 24s on the promise that they would be "mechanically identical" to the Team Lotus cars only to find Chapman's team wheeling out the far more advanced monocoque 25s.

The Lotus 78 and 79 popularized ground-effect aerodynamics in the late 1970s, but other attempts to push the envelope—gas turbine engines, cars with twin chassis—didn't deliver the anticipated results. When Chapman died of a heart attack in 1982, he was only months away from a potential jail sentence for his part in the DeLorean fraud.

It wasn't the front and rear wings that made the Lotus 79 such an innovative, and multiple race and ultimately 1978 championship winning machine; it's the sidepods and under tray that allowed air flow to literally suck the car to the ground. This is Mario Andretti aboard his F1 championship ride.

Qualified Success: The Changing Face of Saturdays ■ ▬▬▬

In the early days of motor racing, grid positions were set by the drivers drawing lots. Practice sessions were just that: practice.

During the prewar era, race promoters began to adopt a system of determining the starting order based on who went quickest during practice. By the time the world championship began in 1950, this had become standard operating procedure.

From 1950 until 1995, the process of setting the grid gradually evolved from taking each driver's best time through practice to establishing two separate sessions, one on Friday and one on Saturday, each dedicated specifically to setting a time. From 1996 onward, F1 began to bend toward the demands of the growing international TV audience, setting aside a single hour on the Saturday afternoon of the race weekend in which each driver had a determined number of laps in which to set a representative time.

But this wasn't good enough. While the principle of having an hour of on-track action packaged for TV was sound, the idea wasn't working out as anticipated. The key problem was track evolution: Over the course of the weekend, as more cars go round the track, they lay an ideal racing line of nice grippy rubber. During qualifying, the big teams would sit and wait, letting others do the work, until the final minutes of the session when the track was theoretically offering more grip. Broadcasters grew increasingly aggravated by the lack of on-track action and lobbied for change.

Through the 2000s, the FIA introduced a succession of tweaks in the hope of ensuring consistent action through the qualifying hour while also making the race itself more exciting. The one-lap format brought in for 2003 was another idea that sounded great in theory but was doomed to failure. On Fridays the cars went out one-by-one to set a lap time that would then determine the running order for Saturday. In that session, the slowest driver from Friday again went first and everybody had to carry the amount of fuel

About the worst thing that can happen in qualifying is to seriously damage the car. This may mean that the car doesn't post a qualifying time and must start at the back of the pack or from the pit lane. In any case, it represents a great deal of work for the pit crew.

F1 drivers, such as Pierre Gasly in the blue shirt and blue jeans are followed constantly by TV crews hoping to get a mini interview or a great quote on the fly. The drivers and teams can love or hate this reality, but it's as much a part of today's Formula 1 as gas, oil, and tires.

Formula 1 Drive to Survive: The Unofficial Companion

with which they planned to start the race. It should have been a win-win: action throughout the hour, TV exposure for the smaller teams, the opportunity to play strategy by running with a light fuel load to get a better grid slot, and ever-present peril in case a driver makes a mistake.

The teams and drivers hated it, complaining that changing weather conditions often made it unfair, and track evolution favored the cars running later. It was tweaked for 2004 and then abandoned in 2005 for a system in which grid positions were set on aggregate times from two different sessions. This was hated so much it was abandoned six races into the season, replaced by a one-shot session in which the running order was determined by finishing positions in the previous race.

In 2006, the FIA rolled out the forerunner of the three-part elimination format, which remains a fixture in grand prix weekends. The first two sessions progressively eliminate the slower drivers until just ten remain in the final shootout for pole. The situation was complicated by various rules related to fuel levels until refueling was banned for 2010, enabling drivers to run with minimal fuel throughout qualifying.

Apart from an ill-fated attempt to introduce eliminations every 90 seconds in 2016 (a format so widely reviled it was abandoned after two rounds), qualifying remained broadly the same until 2021. Under Liberty Media's ownership, F1 has pivoted back toward giving race promoters more opportunities to sell tickets, rather than prioritizing TV. Now a handful of race weekends have qualifying on the Friday; this sets the grid for a short sprint race on Saturday that determines the starting order of Sunday's grand prix.

It remains a work in progress . . .

Another change under Liberty Media's ownership of F1 is that the top three drivers in qualifying now stop in front of the main grandstand to be interviewed in front of the fans.

Anatomy of a Blunder: Abu Dhabi 2021

Depicted in the *Drive to Survive* season 4 finale but not thoroughly explained, the outcome of the 2021 Abu Dhabi Grand Prix and the world championship hung on FIA race director Michael Masi seemingly making up the rules as he went along. Depending on which driver they support, to many fans this was either an outrage or perfectly acceptable.

The facts are that Williams driver Nicholas Latifi crashed into the barrier at turn 14 on lap 53 of 58, causing a safety car. Lewis Hamilton and Max Verstappen were at that point running 1–2, both on hard-compound tires of similar age, but Red Bull took advantage of the safety car to bring Verstappen in for softs. This left him still in second place but now with three lapped cars between him and Hamilton.

F1 sporting regulations have a provision that says that at the end of a safety car period, lapped cars *may* overtake the safety car and rejoin the queue before the race is green flagged. In effect, this enables the race to restart with all the cars in correct position.

Two things went wrong in Abu Dhabi: First, the race director decided to let just three cars—those between Hamilton and Verstappen—unlap themselves; second, he restarted the race a lap earlier than he should have. The first decision was a departure from precedent, but the second actually broke the rules.

Allowing lapped cars to overtake is at the discretion of the race director, but never in F1 history have some rather than all the lapped cars been waved by. The FIA has now changed the wording of the sporting regulations from "any" lapped cars may unlap themselves to "all."

While that previous wording was vague, the rules relating to *when* the race can restart are clear: "at the end of the following lap" after the signal is given for lapped cars to overtake. In Abu Dhabi the three cars were

"Some smile, but nobody laughed." The 2021 F1 championship contest was a season-long, often contentious battle between Red Bull's Max Verstappen (left) and Mercedes-AMG's Lewis Hamilton, and the pot really boiled over at the final, season-deciding race at Abu Dhabi; the on-track battle was intense to say the least, but little more so than the live radio chatter between the team principals and race director. In the end, the winds of spontaneous rules-making administration blew Verstappen's way, giving him his first F1 driver's title.

told to overtake on lap 57, meaning the race should have restarted at the end of lap 58: the final lap. The race would have ended behind the safety car, making Hamilton the world champion. Instead, with the laudable intention of finishing under racing conditions, Masi brought in the safety car and showed the green flag at the end of lap 57. On fresher, softer tires Verstappen had the advantage and duly overtook Hamilton, winning the race and the championship.

Much rancour ensued and lingered well after the *DTS* cameras had stopped rolling. An official FIA investigation described the events of the final laps as "human error," though Masi had "acted in good faith." As well as introducing reworded rules and procedures, the governing body removed Masi from his post.

It was this close as Verstappen pips Hamilton with a final pass at the 2021 season ender in Abu Dhabi.

Grin and bear it. Verstappen and Hamilton muster up a semi-smile and a handshake after one of the most hotly contest, and contentious, F1 championship finales in history. It certainly couldn't have been easy for Lewis Hamilton, as he lost this particular battle and the 2021 season's title war.

Formula 1 Drive to Survive: The Unofficial Companion

As chief mechanic at Brabham, Charlie Whiting worked with one of the most creative engineers in the business—Gordon Murray—and knew all the tricks teams played with the rules. After Bernie Ecclestone sold the team and moved full-time into superintending F1's commercial rights, he arranged for Whiting to take a job as the FIA's technical delegate, presiding over the legality of all the cars in competition and keeping the technical rule book up to date. In 1997 he became the race director and safety delegate, as well as the individual in charge of starting each race. It was Whiting who decided to change to the present start-light system. After years of noting from his trackside perch that drivers weren't waiting for the green lights to come on, but were anticipating when the red lights went out, he realized the green lights were pointless. The length of time between the row of five lights switching on completely and then going off is now randomized.

Whiting suffered a fatal pulmonary embolism three days before the 2019 Australian Grand Prix.

The late Charlie Whiting smiles big aboard a Mercedes-AMG SLS F1 safety car. He was more than well equipped to act as the FIA's chief rules gatekeeper, given his previous experience a chief mechanic at Brabham F1, under the clever and innovative Gordon Murray. Over time he also served as an F1 race director, safety delegate, and official starter.

Changes for the 2009 season sought to reduce overall downforce levels with a view to improving overtaking. The FIA even set up an Overtaking Working Group involving the teams to formulate these rules. What wasn't known at the time was that three parties at the table had found a way of "legally" flouting the rules they were helping to create.

Among the new regulations was a limitation on the size of diffusers, the shaped venturi on the floor between the rear wheels. These work by accelerating airflow through the area, generating a low-pressure zone below the car. Curtailing their size therefore cuts potential downforce (in theory).

The rules were phrased poorly, describing how any intersecting surfaces should form "one continuous line which is visible from beneath the car." This meant the diffuser, which is a three-dimensional form, needed to be legal in only one dimension. Three teams spotted the loophole and exploited it by fitting their diffusers with a second deck that considerably expanded its effective volume. Toyota even fitted a third deck during the season.

Other teams disputed the legality of these designs, but they were allowed to continue, only being banned at the end of the season.

Rear wing and diffuser designs are closely watched and measured by F1's scrutineers as this is an area where teams have purposely, or accidentally, cheated the rules in the past. This is the 2022 season McLaren MCL36.

An inordinate amount of time and effort goes into policing F1 aerodynamic devices; unfortunately for the FIA, there was for a time an ambiguously worded rules passage that gave teams considerable bandwidth to "optimize" their rear wings and diffusers—not overtly blatant cheating, but enough of a brouhaha to initiate a rewording of the technical rules at the end of the 2009 season, to fully clarify the intent and wording of the rule.

Rule Benders

The Secret Fuel Tank

Postrace, F1 cars are weighed with their fuel tanks empty to ensure they meet the minimum weight limit and that teams haven't been using fuel as ballast.

The 2005 San Marino Grand Prix had a peculiar aftermath: BAR driver Jenson Button, who had finished third, was deleted from the results when his car was found to be 5 kilograms underweight after the race. The scrutineers had located and drained a mysterious auxiliary fuel tank before weighing the car.

While BAR managed to get this decision overturned on a technicality, the FIA launched an investigation and decided the device represented a clear attempt to run the car below the weight limit during the race, then ballast it up to the correct figure before going on the weighbridge. The team was stripped of its Imola points and banned for two races.

Jenson Button aboard his BAR Honda F1 machine at San Marino in 2005, when the team was caught running an illegal fuel tank device and stripped of its points and given a two-race suspension.

In a similar dodge to BAR-Honda's illegal
fuel tank, the Tyrrell team ran their 012
car underweight during the 1984 season,
adding lead ballast during late-race pit
stops under the pretext of topping up engine
coolant. While this wasn't specifically
forbidden, the team were thrown out of the
world championship anyway on the trumped-up
charge of using illegal fuel additives.

Chapter 6

MONEY GAME

THE BUSINESS OF F1

Money makes the Formula 1 world go round. But there hasn't always been enough of it to go around. The battle between the teams to secure the money to go racing is almost as intense as the action on track—and sometimes it's a fight just to stay in business . . .

We don't know for sure if the cost of Pierre Gasly's pair of 2019 preseason practice crashes cost him his seat on the front line Red Bull squad, prompting his reassignment to the sister AlphaTauri team; no matter, it worked out well enough for both sides of the equation, as Red Bull went on to win the F1 title in 2021 and Gasly bagged his first F1 win aboard an AlphaTauri.

If You're Not First, You're Last

"Finishing seventh, eighth, ninth has no value to us." Red Bull team principal Christian Horner's words during S2:E5 of *Drive to Survive* are considered so important to the narrative that they're repeated during the following episode. And they carry a fundamental truth about modern Formula 1: Results have a direct effect on a team's earnings.

Only the top ten finishers in each grand prix score points. At the end of the season a portion of F1's commercial revenues is divided up among the teams according to their position in the constructors' championship, with the majority shares going to those further up. The differences between those finishing positions can be counted in tens of millions of dollars.

The cost of competition is staggering. Elsewhere in that *Drive to Survive* episode, "Great Expectations," Horner puts the cost of Pierre Gasly's two crashes during preseason testing at $2 million. For a team of Red Bull's size and resources, that is a mere dent—what exercised Horner more greatly was that the crashes left his team short on spares at an important point of the season.

Throughout the existence of the world championship, the competitive picture of F1 has been bent out of shape by economic inequalities. Aside from a few high-profile exceptions, the wealthiest teams generally produce the best cars and can afford to hire the fastest drivers. The most successful teams also attract the juiciest sponsorship deals on top of whatever they earn from the prize fund. While IT company Cognizant is believed to pay around $30 million a season to sponsor the mid-grid Aston Martin, the chemicals giant Ineos took a 33 percent stake in multiple world champions Mercedes in a transaction estimated to be over $800 million.

The frontrunners also amass enough political influence to protect their own interests.

Betting and bookmaking are the least of the money issues underpinning Formula 1. The costs of running a team is high, as are the costs of operating an F1 racing circuit—TV contracts and team sponsorships ring up some of the biggest dollars in sports and business marketing.

While running in the tenth position on track might satisfy lesser F1 teams, such a finishing placement means nothing to today's top line teams like Mercedes-AMG, Ferrari, and Red Bull.

Since 2021 all F1 teams have had to operate within a budget cap, initially set at $145 million per year. Reaching a consensus on this was a painfully drawn-out process: The smaller teams wanted it set lower because they weren't earning enough to spend that much, while the money-no-object organizations at the front of the grid fought against the entire principle because it meant making painful cuts. It was the economic circumstances of the pandemic that drove a final agreement to disagree. Three teams nearly went bust and even Liberty Media, who paid $4.6 billion for F1's commercial rights in 2017, had to resort to a little financial engineering to keep its shareholders happy. A compromise was found in the form of a new Concorde Agreement (see page 156), which distributed income more fairly and enshrined the principle of the budget cap. Rather than let talented staff go, Red Bull and Mercedes transferred people to newly established advanced technology businesses, which offered engineering services for hire; Ferrari seconded many of their staff to their closely aligned engine customers, Haas and Alfa Romeo. Crisis averted.

Liberty Media's next task is to adapt to the changing circumstances of the global market. The previous regime led by Bernie Ecclestone brought in huge sums of cash, amounting to around 70 percent of total revenue, from two major sources: TV rights and race sanctioning fees. The Chinese government, for instance, spent $240 million constructing its circuit in Shanghai (which was built on reclaimed swampland and rests on over 40,000 concrete piles sunk into the ground) and reportedly paid $50 million per year for the privilege of hosting a race. These are unsustainable sums, well beyond what an ordinary business (e.g., a professional race promoter) could afford. And while the well of countries wanting to put themselves on the global sporting map in this way is starting to run low, F1 still hasn't quite hit bottom: Azerbaijan, Qatar, and Saudi Arabia recently signed up to $55 million deals. Ecclestone left a tangled mess of arrangements that Liberty is working through—Monaco, for instance, is believed to pay just $15 million per year *and* retains the very lucrative rights to trackside advertising. But Liberty has also shown it's willing to bend if the market is important enough—to have new GPs in the USA, in Miami and Las Vegas, Liberty effectively went into partnership with the race promoters.

Likewise, that other Ecclestone-era cash cow, TV rights, faces a potentially turbulent future as more viewers cut the cord and embrace streaming services. F1's migration to pay-TV platforms in the past couple of decades came at a cost in terms of audience growth, but it raked in huge sums. Liberty's most lucrative contract is the deal to broadcast to the UK; Sky TV emerged victorious from a bidding war in 2019, agreeing to pay $255 million per year until 2024. The company has its own channel devoted to F1 and sends a huge cast of personnel to each grand prix, including expert pundits such as 1996 world champion Damon Hill and 2009 champion Jenson Button. Liberty has established its own streaming platform, F1 TV, but has had to tread carefully (and geo-lock it in certain territories) to avoid alienating some major sources of income.

Having funded the acquisition of the commercial rights through debt, Liberty *has* to keep expanding the F1 business to bring more money in. That means more races, more competition for trackside signage—and, given its role in popularizing F1 in the USA, more seasons of *Drive to Survive*.

One other thing is for sure: The teams will want their share of whatever rewards come from that growth. In an environment where costs are capped but income isn't and challengers are effectively barred from entry (under the latest Concorde Agreement, any team wanting to join the grid must pay a $200 million fee), teams are in charge of their commercial destiny almost as never before. Little wonder McLaren CEO Zak Brown has said that by the end of the 2020s teams will have become billion-dollar franchises.

McLaren CEO Zak Brown believes F1 teams will have become multi billion dollar franchises by the end of the 2020s under the new commercial arrangements. None of them have got there yet…

"Power couple" Bernie Ecclestone and Michael
Schumacher ruled Formula 1 for a generation.
Ecclestone has given up his position as one
of F1's most influential ringmasters, and
seven-time F1 champ Schumacher is retired.

Formula 1 Drive to Survive: The Unofficial Companion

Drive to Survive likes to side with the underdog. In the first series it juxtaposes Force India/Racing Point teammates Esteban Ocon and Sergio Pérez as they fight to retain their seats, the implication being that Pérez emerges the unworthy winner purely because he brings sponsorship, whereas the talented but penniless Ocon doesn't. But there isn't necessarily an inverse relationship between money and talent (indeed, *DTS* is highly economical with the truth—Ocon was in Mercedes' junior driver program and got his place with Force India as part of a deal in which they received Mercedes engines at a discount).

In August 1991 nobody would have picked Michael Schumacher as a future seven-time world champion. Sure, he was quick in a Mercedes sportscar, but so were his teammates. It took $150,000 of Mercedes cash to get him into F1.

The Jordan team (now racing as Aston Martin, several changes of owner later) had a hole to fill and bills to pay. Despite performing remarkably well in their maiden year, they were behind on payments to several creditors (including engine supplier Cosworth). And one of their drivers was on his way to jail after spraying a London taxi driver with CS gas, or tear gas, during a road-rage incident.

So there were plenty of items competing for priority on team boss Eddie Jordan's to-do list, right after the big one of how to tell the sponsors. Jordan had picked up several points finishes in recent races and stood to earn a share of F1's commercial revenues through placing well in the constructors' championship at the end of the year. But Eddie needed money immediately. So who to recruit—a veteran who would perhaps be more likely to rack up points, but who would want to be paid, or a rookie who would pay for the privilege of driving?

The short-term need for cold, hard cash won out. Jordan took Mercedes' $150,000 and the rest is history. Schumacher qualified seventh for the Belgian Grand Prix, only to break his clutch at the start, but he'd done enough to attract attention. Sadly for Jordan, in the rush to get the deal done in time for Spa, certain contractual details were left up in the air—and Schumacher found himself driving a Benetton next time out. F1 ringmaster Bernie Ecclestone, spotting Schumacher's potential to energize the German audience, orchestrated the move from a team closer to the front of the grid.

McLaren boss Ron Dennis commiserated with the disconsolate Eddie Jordan, saying, "Welcome to the Piranha Club."

> ## " IN AUGUST 1991 NOBODY WOULD HAVE PICKED MICHAEL SCHUMACHER AS A FUTURE SEVEN-TIME WORLD CHAMPION."

Concorde Discord

The contract between the teams, F1, and the FIA is top secret. It takes its name not from the supersonic passenger aircraft but from the location where the first agreement was thrashed out over the course of a touchy day-long session in January 1981: the FIA's headquarters on the Place de la Concorde in Paris, France.

Control over F1's rules and its commercial arrangements was at stake. On one side was the FIA's sporting committee and its president, Jean-Marie Balestre; on the other, the Formula One Constructors' Association (FOCA), a body representing the majority of privately owned teams and led by Brabham owner Bernie Ecclestone and his legal advisor, Max Mosley. FOCA felt it received an unfairly small share of the commercial proceeds of F1, and that the FIA kept making up rules on the fly, which favored the big manufacturer teams. The ongoing dispute had led to boycotts and races either being cancelled or declared ineligible for championship points. It was beginning to make F1 uninvestable, and key sponsors and suppliers were wavering.

Imagine watching *Drive to Survive* and seeing entire teams randomly appear and disappear between episodes.

Among the key concessions of the first Concorde Agreement was the granting of the TV rights to FOCA, initially under a short lease agreement. Until this point TV coverage had been piecemeal, because broadcasters weren't necessarily interested in F1 and promoters feared the effects on ticket sales. But under the new contract, teams agreed to compete in every race on the calendar or face being thrown out of the championship. This gave Ecclestone a stable package to offer broadcasters—and, being a gifted dealmaker, he made the most of it.

What had initially seemed to be the crumbs brushed from the commercial table became a veritable goldmine. In subsequent years, Ecclestone would step away from team ownership, FOCA would morph into the

As if to say, "Hit the road, Max," it's difficult to imagine that these two (Max Mosley, left, and Bernie Ecclestone) didn't clash now and again (and also accomplish a lot for the sport). Less of their work and clashes seemed to involve the racing, with more of them fashioned around the many money aspects of Formula 1, such as team payouts, sponsorship, and massive television rights and contracts.

commercial entity we know today as the Formula One Group, and the amount to which Ecclestone was enriching himself became increasingly contentious. In the mid-1990s, with Mosley now FIA president and seemingly working hand-in-glove with Ecclestone, teams began to object—especially when it was revealed Ecclestone had transferred the commercial rights to a trust in his wife's name, protected from scrutiny by a Russian doll network of offshore companies.

Subsequent iterations of the Concorde Agreement were subject to even more protracted arguments than the original—taking months and years, rather than hours or days, to settle. Now Mosley and Ecclestone were the establishment the teams were fighting against, and it's ironic that on Ecclestone's watch the inequalities and unfairness grew.

One of Liberty Media's most significant achievements since acquiring the commercial rights was the signing of a new Concorde Agreement in 2020, sweeping away the legacy of Ecclestone's divide-and-rule tactics, which had left almost half the grid impoverished and with no say in rule making. The new contract divided the commercial revenue more equitably as well as enshrining each team with a franchise value.

Peace now rules in F1—or so it seems . . .

" NOW MOSLEY AND ECCLESTONE WERE THE ESTABLISHMENT THE TEAMS WERE FIGHTING AGAINST"

For a time, this was the FIA, F1, and the FOCA's power triumvirate (from left): Jean Marie Balestre, Max Mosley, and Bernie Ecclestone.

Eddie Irvine, former teammate of Michael
Schumacher, was Jaguar Racing's lead driver
and one of Ford's highest-paid employees.
And his ultimate boss didn't know who he
was or what he did.

In motorsport circles there's a cliché that is no less true for being oft repeated: the quickest way to make a small fortune in motor racing is to start off with a large one. Money alone is no guarantee of success: it's not just what you have, but how you spend it.

Toyota spent eight seasons in F1 without a single victory to its name despite employing several high-profile drivers and engineers. In fact, Toyota was so desperate to poach Renault technical director Mike Gascoyne in 2003 that it included use of a private jet in the deal so he could commute to work at the team's base in Cologne, Germany, without moving home from the UK. When Gascoyne's tenure ended, his tale was a familiar one of constant interference from big-corporation apparatchiks with no understanding of motor racing. During his final months there, he kept a radio-controlled model tank in his office with a functional cap gun, which he used to fire at corporate functionaries he didn't like.

While the Ford Motor Company's dalliances with F1 haven't been uniformly disastrous— they bankrolled development of the Cosworth V-8 engine, which democratized power from the 1960s through to the early 1990s—its acquisition of a team ranks among F1's most humiliating failures. As with Toyota, it is a tale of pointless profligacy, corporate hubris, and a revolving door of senior managers best summed up by one infamous quotation.

Ford bought the Stewart team at the end of 1999 and rebranded it as Jaguar Racing, a pure marketing exercise for one of FoMoCo's luxury brands. Stewart had won a grand prix, but, over the course of the next five seasons, Jaguar failed to come close to matching that achievement despite taking on the same facilities and staff (many of whom left or were driven out in various corporate coups).

Late in 2001, against a background of declining market share and high-profile lawsuits relating to tire failures on the Explorer model, William Clay Ford Jr., great-grandson of the founder, became the chief executive with a mandate to make massive cost cuts. A look at the payroll revealed the name of an individual who was being paid $10 million a year to do . . . Ford knew not what.

The usually animated, yet in this photo quite pensive, Irish F1 and sports car racer Eddie Irvine ably withstood the pressure of being Michael Schumacher's Ferrari teammate and won four Grands Prix in his own right.

Bargaining Power

Before F1's revenues were dispensed from a central pot, it was up to teams to negotiate their rewards with individual race promoters. While prize money was usually billed publicly and well in advance, starting money—in effect an appearance fee—was different for every entrant, and usually depended on their box-office potential. Famous names enabled the promoters to sell more tickets, after all.

That began to change as F1 races became more widely televised in the 1960s and '70s, and Bernie Ecclestone in effect unionized the teams to negotiate as a block. Ecclestone, a former motorcycle dealer, had been in and out of motor racing as a driver manager and wheeler-dealer before buying the Brabham team in 1971. He formed the Formula One Constructors' Association (FOCA) to push for better deals, uniting the predominantly British-based teams who built their own chassis and ran virtually identical Ford-Cosworth V-8 engines. Manufacturer teams and the likes of Enzo Ferrari were sometimes allied, sometimes not, depending on the prevailing political winds. The advent of the Concorde Agreement (see page 156) brought relative stability and set F1 on the way to its present form as a TV spectacle with a consistent set of entrants from race to race.

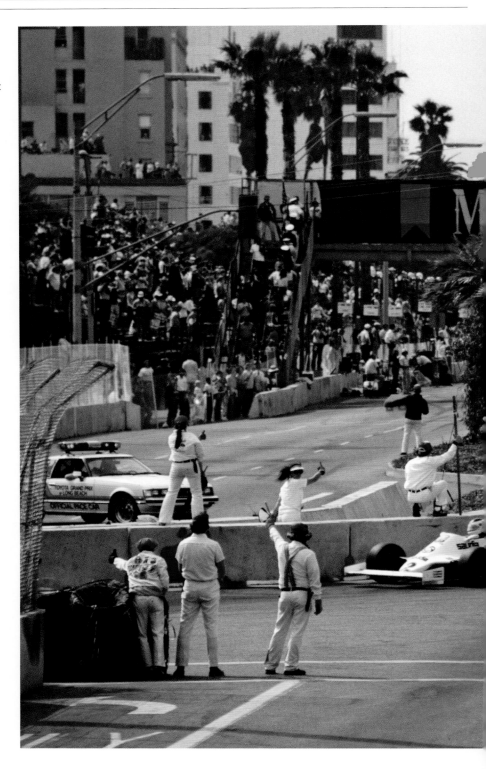

Bernie Ecclestone's efforts effectively allowed smaller private teams to negotiate as a block with larger works teams. Here two of those smaller teams, Williams and Ecclestone's Brabham, run one-two at the U.S. Grand Prix West in 1981, the year of the Concorde Agreement.

Cash Is King

Ayrton Senna and the Coin Flip

Racing drivers are as competitive with each other over money as they are over who is fastest on track. Some rely on their managers to negotiate, others employ companies to look after their affairs, while some relish the challenge of a hard negotiation as much as they'd look forward to going wheel-to-wheel with a key rival on track.

The saga of Ayrton Senna's bitter rivalry with McLaren teammate Alain Prost in the late 1980s has become legendary. Less well-known are the circumstances behind Senna's move to that team in the first place. He knew they had the best car. McLaren boss Ron Dennis knew Senna couldn't resist the

opportunity. And yet neither of them could agree on Senna's salary. The difference between what Senna wanted per year and what Dennis was willing to pay was a not-insignificant sum: $500,000.

Desperate to resolve the impasse but unwilling—perhaps for his own ego-related reasons—to concede ground, Dennis suggested they flip a coin. Senna's limited grasp of English meant he couldn't understand the concept of "heads or tails" until it was written down; in fact, they spent a further 5 minutes refining the protocol of the coin flip, right down to what would happen if it got landed on its side in the office's deep-pile

carpet. Dennis won the toss—and only then remembered they were agreeing on a three-year contract.

The coin flip had been worth $1.5 million.

No misunderstanding or coin flipping here as Ayrton Senna (left) and then McLaren Team boss Ron Dennis celebrate their 1993 Monaco Grand Prix win each with a trophy to carry home. Senna is considered among the greatest "masters of Monaco" with a record six victories to his credit.

Ayrton Senna da Silva will go down in
history as among the greatest F1 drivers.
Often criticized for some of his roughhouse
driving, his car control was incomparable.
Senna earned three world championships
and forty-one wins during his ten-year
F1 career.

" THE COIN FLIP HAD BEEN WORTH $1.5 MILLION."

Wealth and desperation coexist in Formula 1. It's a cash-hungry business in which many teams have struggled to stay in existence. This involves kissing a few frogs. Spend long enough in F1 and you'll see sponsors and wannabe team owners come and go, some more quickly than expected, leaving a mess behind.

The perceived wealth and glamour of F1 acts as a magnet to chancers. Often it's the case that they have *some* money, enough to make the first couple of payment installments, and they believe that once they've gained admission to the F1 paddock they can begin doing further deals, which will bring cash flooding in. This ambition is rarely realized. During the lifetime of *Drive to Survive*, two tail-end teams, Haas and Williams, have had title sponsors default on payments. The saga of Rich Energy and Haas is covered in S2:E2 of *DTS*, and the program makers are peculiarly favorable to a sponsor whose own publicly available financial records revealed a bank balance that barely stretched to tens of dollars let alone millions.

At least no actual criminality was involved in these deals. Had Netflix been around in the 1980s, it would have been fascinating to see how it portrayed the likes of Joachim Luthi and Jean-Pierre Van Rossem, two aspiring team owners who were rogues of the highest order. Luthi, a Swiss banker, bought the Brabham team in 1989 but shortly afterwards went on the run, charged with embezzling $133 million from his investors.

The bearded, wild-haired Van Rossem also spent barely a year in F1, during which he managed to enrage both Bernie Ecclestone and the president of the FIA (by calling a press conference in which he described them as a mafioso and a Nazi sympathizer). Van Rossem had already done time for fraud when he arrived in the F1 paddock as the sponsor and new majority owner of the tiny Onyx team. He had outspoken opinions about how F1 should be run, but he also had boundless reserves of money—or so it seemed. Van Rossem had reinvented himself in the greed-is-good '80s as a stock market guru and the inventor of Moneytron, a top-secret supercomputer that had the power to predict stock market movements. His investors included the Belgian royal family.

Van Rossem got as far as nearly (but not quite) agreeing an engine-supply deal with Porsche (he supposedly burned one of his Porsches in protest when the arrangement fell through). When Moneytron was revealed as a Ponzi scheme, he was on his way to jail again. New majority owner Peter Monteverdi proved to be almost as eccentric, firing the technical director and installing himself as chief engineer.

Such are the hazards of being a back-of-the-grid team.

" WEALTH AND DESPERATION COEXIST IN FORMULA 1."

Durex Condoms is among the more controversial, or at least most joked about, sponsors in F1 history—although the company did nothing wrong by producing a legal product and wanting to advertise it to an international audience. One can only hope that the performance of the product exceeded that of this Surtees TS19 that carried its logo and colors.

Chapter 7

THINK FAST

F1 STRATEGY

Often talked about, but little understood, F1 strategy is an exercise in managing complexity and risk, and juggling different probabilities. At the beginning of a race, anything can happen; in the closing stages, all the different permutations converge toward a single outcome. The winner is often the team that makes the best calls under changing circumstances.

F1 pit stops are an explosive display of color and motion. The car needs to enter the correct pit box, come to a full stop, be jacked into the air, and have all four tires changed, in fewer than 2.5 seconds. This is possible because F1 currently doesn't require refueling, which has come and gone from the F1 pit formula before. Any additional repairs or aerodynamic adjustments generally add to the desired low to mid 2-second stop time. A bungled tire change can, and has, cost any given team the difference between a win and a midpack finish.

It Starts with Data

Drive to Survive loves the drama of pit stops but shies away from the granular detail of strategy. That's partly because the program makers feel the subject may be too complex for casual viewers, but also because even though teams are more open with the *DTS* crew than any other media, strategic operations remain top secret.

Every F1 car carries a GPS tracker and around 300 sensors that monitor everything from suspension movement and g-forces to the engine's health and how hard the driver is pushing the brake pedal. All this data—up to three or four gigabytes during a race—is transmitted back to the pit wall and then on to the factory, where the leading teams have special rooms staffed by math specialists who help make strategic calls on the fly. F1 also has trackside sensors, which it uses to augment the TV coverage with live data and strategic predictions made by its partner, Amazon Web Services.

Each turn of the wheel adds fidelity to strategic models the teams have been building since before they arrived at the circuit. Back at the factory, every team has a "driver-in-the-loop" simulator room where they evaluate the effect on lap time of different mechanical setups (ride height, suspension stiffness, wing settings, and so on), and start to get a handle on how long the tires might last based on performance data. At the track, they build on that data set by observing whether the virtual testing is reflected in real life. The key questions are: How fast can we go, and for how long, before the tires wear out or degrade?

Based on this information, the strategists build potential scenarios of how many pit stops they're likely to make, and

The team's computerized telemetry readouts are custom for every race and every track. They provide a dizzying amount of real-time data, able to let the team (and driver) know if their race is proceding according to the strategy plan or not, and guiding adjustments as needed.

The job of team managers and strategists isn't to watch the race or the track; it's to monitor the real-time data flow from the car and the driver's track position and performance in order to craft a winning strategy.

when, and how they might respond to what rivals do. All these scenarios are underpinned by data because gambling on outcomes is viewed as fundamentally bad practice, even if the outcome is successful.

Chief strategists generally come from a combined math/engineering background at prestigious educational establishments. Alfa Romeo's Ruth Buscombe received an honors degree in aerospace and aerothermal engineering at Cambridge University, for instance, while McLaren's Randeep Singh was an honors student in engineering and management at Oxford. Both also wrote the strategy software their teams rely on.

Whatever preordained scenarios teams run through before the race, they still need to monitor and react while the cars are on track. There are several key inputs in these decisions, chiefly tire performance and longevity, but also on-track incidents and the position of other cars on the track. To enable quick decision-making, strategists have a

simple graphic onscreen view of the track as a circle, showing the gap to the cars behind: knowing how long a pit stop is likely to take enables them to predict whether their driver will emerge from the pitlane with a clear track ahead or with cars potentially blocking the way.

F1 drivers train, practice, and learn new circuits on highly sophisticated simulators, far and beyond the ones you'll find in game shops and car dealerships.

Talk about laser focussed—check out the gaze on Alfa Romeo's Chief Strategist engineer Ruth Buscombe, at right. Team driver Antonio Giovanazzi is at left, with chief trackside engineer Zevi Pujolar middle. Ms. Buscombe is highly educated and triply qualified for this position, and only one of many women in senior engineering positions in F1.

Think Fast: F1 Strategy

You Only Know What You Know

F1 strategy is process driven rather than outcome driven. That's why reporters and fans often see races differently than the strategists. It's easy to fall into the trap of judging strategic decisions based on outcome alone. And as the cliché goes, hindsight is always 20/20.

No matter how many strategic simulations teams run through prerace, unpredictable weather, as one example, can toss the plans in the trash heap. Even the leading teams can be totally undone by randomness. Mercedes provided a case study of this in the 2019 German Grand Prix, chronicled in S2:E4 of *Drive to Survive*.

On the weekend, as the team were celebrating their parent company's 125 years in motor racing, a heatwave in central Europe broke overnight into thunderstorms and intermittently torrential rain. Mercedes drivers Lewis Hamilton and Valtteri Bottas led the early stages of the race on a gradually drying track, but a series of crashes and mechanical retirements elsewhere on the circuit, along with another downpour, proved their undoing.

Mercedes appeared to have got most of their calls right in the early phases while Red Bull seemed to be in trouble, putting Max Verstappen on dry-weather tires too early. He spun and came back for intermediate tires.

Where Mercedes came unglued was in the chaos around the second safety car. Ferrari's Charles Leclerc spun at the penultimate corner and got stuck in the gravel, prompting the safety car; when Hamilton arrived, he also went off there, but was able to rejoin the track minus his front wing. He then dived into the pits, but shortcut the entry lane and picked up a penalty for doing so. Worse still, his pit crew, which was expecting Bottas, hadn't had time to prepare.

Another opportunity seemed lost with a later safety car period. With the track drying, Mercedes delayed pitting both drivers for slicks again. Had they done so earlier, the penalty Hamilton served would have been less costly. This was all rendered moot as both drivers then spun on the still-slippery track.

The rain that impacted 2019 German Grand Prix resulted in a tumultuous race, to say the least.

A bad day for Mercedes, but one that looks worse in hindsight. Something similar could be said for McLaren, which lost an opportunity to put Carlos Sainz on the podium by not pitting him for slicks during the final safety car deployment. He finished fifth, leapfrogged by Toro Rosso's Daniil Kvyat and Racing Point's Lance Stroll, who did take on slicks behind the safety car.

While this made Toro Rosso and Racing Point's strategists look supersharp, it was a huge gamble because the weather radar (and the sky) suggested more rain was imminent. As it was, reporters purringly described it as "an inspired gamble." Had the heavens opened at that point, hindsight would have judged the call more harshly.

Mercedes flagellated themselves after the race, but much of what happened was a matter of luck. Verstappen went relatively unpunished for spinning and stopping again, since he didn't damage his car, while Hamilton did—and then brought more problems upon himself by missing the pit entry and catching his team unprepared.

The point that can be lost on viewers of a TV show with a narrative arc is that races never pan out exactly as planned because random events get in the way. That's why strategists rate the quality of their decisions according to what they knew at the time, and why they generally *react* to rain rather than trying to preempt its arrival. Wet-weather tires wear out fast on a dry surface. The "crossover point"—when a track is just about dry enough for slick tires—is tough to predict, and usually based on driver feel rather than hard data.

Like trying to time the stock market, you only hit the perfect moment by accident—but you look very clever if you do.

Lewis Hamilton enjoys the Landaulet seating in this outsized Mercedes-Benz 600 limo during the drivers' parade ahead of the 2019 German Grand Prix. This is about as good as Merc's celebration of its 125 years in motor racing got…

125 Years Motorsport

Tires: It's Complicated

While some media organizations cover every practice session as slavishly as if it were a race in itself, the casual viewer might wonder at the point of it all. Cars go out, cover a few laps, maybe not even fast ones, then come in again. So what?

But every second of track time counts in these sessions, not just in terms of dialing in the cars' suspension and aerodynamic setups, but also in understanding what strategic options the tires are going to give.

In past eras the presence of multiple tire suppliers complicated the picture and led to costly technological wars. Pirelli has been F1's sole tire supplier since 2011 and was given a very strange brief: to make every race like the 2010 Canadian Grand Prix. This was a race where several factors, including a partially resurfaced track and cooler-than-expected temperatures, caused tire issues that led to multiple pit stops and a fantastically unpredictable race. Bernie Ecclestone, the F1 rights holder at the time, effectively told Pirelli, "More of the same, please."

Ecclestone's demand has shaped grand prix racing ever since. Pirelli has tried to produce tires that operate perfectly up to a point, and then degrade rapidly (but safely), theoretically opening multiple strategic opportunities.

It's important that we separate degradation from wear. F1 tires don't wear out like road car tires; they just reach a point where the chemical reaction that enables them to stick to the track surface is spent, and they lose grip. This can happen for a number of reasons, and it's why you'll often hear drivers griping to their race engineer about their tires: push the rubber too hard, too soon, and it can overheat and damage the surface. There's also a distinct operating temperature "window"—until the tire reaches this, it offers little grip at all.

Tire choice is a key strategic decision. There are three specs of tire available for each race, now simply labeled soft, medium, and hard (there are actually five different tire types, to suit all the circuits on the calendar, but for simplicity sake the three selected compounds follow the same naming rubric). In theory the softest has the most grip but the shortest life.

Here's where the math is involved: What lap times can you achieve on each compound, and how consistently? How long will they last? How many pit stops will you have to make? Tire performance varies among drivers, cars, and circuits. Some cars are harder on tires than others (conversely, cars that are too gentle may struggle to "switch on" their tires by getting them into the operating window mentioned previously); some drivers are better at keeping their tires in the sweet spot; and some tracks have more abrasive surfaces, or layouts that punish one particular corner of the car.

The ideal strategy, barring incident, is one in which the car completes the distance in the shortest possible time. That means the fastest combination of tires with the fewest possible stops. That's why a lot of the running during Friday practice is devoted to race simulations—so the team can get a handle on which is the best tire for the track and conditions.

Members of the Haas team prepare tires before a race. There are three specs of tire available for each race, now simply labeled soft, medium, and hard. In theory the softest has the most grip but the shortest life.

" TIRE CHOICE IS A KEY STRATEGIC DECISION."

Track Position Is King

The basic F1 strategy is to preserve whatever advantage you have over all the cars behind you. There's almost a throwaway moment in the *Drive to Survive* S1:E8 in which Alfa Romeo chief strategist Ruth Buscombe reminds Marcus Ericsson that one of the most important factors in his race is going to be "track position."

Despite changes to the sport, such as the change to Pirelli tires mandated by Bernie Ecclestone as mentioned previously, it remains hard to overtake in Formula 1. Therefore, it's important for a driver to put themselves into a position where they don't have to do it. It's also vital for the strategists who make the pit calls.

Monaco is the perfect example of a circuit where track position is key. You don't want to give it up by going into the pits, so the fewer pit stops the better. But timing is also important. If you come out of the pits behind another car, you lose more time than if you were running on a clear track. This gives rivals an opportunity to pounce.

Track position also can neutralize the advantage of running on different tire strategies.

In the 2021 Bahrain Grand Prix depicted in *Drive to Survive* S4:E1, Max Verstappen qualified on pole and led the early stages of the race ahead of Lewis Hamilton. Although Verstappen was able to stretch his first set of tires four laps longer than Hamilton, he emerged from that pit stop behind the Mercedes. After their final stops, Verstappen had tires ten laps fresher than Hamilton's and was theoretically quicker, but got only one good chance to overtake, and overran the track limits when he did, forcing him to give the position back.

"Clearly today track position was key again," concluded Max.

Track position (in other words, a car's position in the race relative to the leader's) is always critical to a variety of strategy decisions but particularly so in the case of a tight, twisty course where it's difficult to pass and gain positions, such as historic Monaco.

On-track traffic jams can become racing
accidents on tight tracks such as Monaco.
Notice that the damaged Williams at
foreground left has already come to a stop
while the Ferrari it came in contact with
is still airborn.

Pit Stops: High-Speed Ballet

In keeping with the idea that the winner is the driver who covers the race distance in the shortest possible time, pit stops need to be as short as possible. Time spent dawdling in the pits is time wasted.

In the early days of grand prix racing and the world championship, equipment was so primitive that teams and drivers preferred to avoid stopping at all unless the car needed fuel or tires or the driver needed a drink (more common than you might think in the days when races could last 3 hours or more). Minutes could be wasted jacking the car up and removing wheels, or sloshing fuel into the tank with a huge can and a funnel. Even as late as the 1970s, pit stops weren't exactly leisurely, but they lacked choreography.

The Brabham team put tactical pit stops on the table in 1982 when they began factoring a midrace fuel stop into their plans, believing a lighter car could run faster. It all hinged on

Ready and waiting; at this point, the driver must hit his marks and stop perfectly within his pit box for all the hands and equipment to have proper access to the car.

Today's pitside wheel gun is a highly sophisticated piece of equipment; a far cry from the days when tires used to be changed with a hammer beating on a knockoff central wheel nut. The gun not only does the tire job, but notifies a monitoring system when its job is done for that stop.

 Strategy in Action

Pit Games

One of the most basic strategic plays is the "undercut," used to great effect by Ferrari in the early 2000s: Your driver pits first, then is fast enough on their first lap out of the pits to leapfrog their rival for position when they make their stop. The opposite of this is the "overcut," where your driver pits later and is faster during the crucial lap where their rival leaves the pits. Success or failure with these tactics depends on several factors:

for instance, time spent delayed by other cars, pit stop mishaps, how out-of-shape the old tires are, and how long the new ones take to come up to working temperature.

Given that every pit crew member is protected with a full racing style fire suit, shoes, anda helmet, it's hard to imagine that in the past, some pit crews wore short sleeve shirts, short pants, and no helmet—even during the eras of refuelling.

whether time gained through running light outweighed time lost in the pits. Clearly it worked—they won the world championship in '83 and were competitive in '82—but the practice was banned for the 1984 season because of the risk of fire.

Midrace refueling was reintroduced in 1984, but with strict controls on the technology, which now incorporated the type of couplings used to refuel aircraft inflight. Even then, the Benetton team was caught tampering with its equipment to increase the fuel flow, revealed when the car of Jos Verstappen (father of Max) went up in flames after a spill in the German Grand Prix.

Ferrari exploited the strategic possibilities of refueling during their remarkable run in the early 2000s. They deliberately built their cars with smaller fuel tanks, confident that by stopping more often, and at the right time, they could essentially overtake their rivals in the pits.

Refueling was banned again for 2010, but this only led to a new technological arms race. Before, the length of the stop was dictated by how much fuel was put in the car, because it could only flow at a prescribed rate. Now the only limit on stop length was how fast you could change the wheels and tires. In response, teams drilled their pit crews harder, often sending them to bootcamps, and developed bespoke equipment that could operate faster.

The result was pit stops of fewer than 3 seconds rather than of eight or more. Teams shaved further fractions of a second by cutting out the human factor: Now a light rather than a person holding a sign signals the driver to leave the pit, and the mechanics press a button on the wheel gun to signal their task is complete rather than putting their hands in the air.

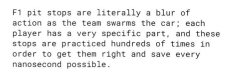

F1 pit stops are literally a blur of action as the team swarms the car; each player has a very specific part, and these stops are practiced hundreds of times in order to get them right and save every nanosecond possible.

Formula 1 Drive to Survive: The Unofficial Companion

Drive to Survive likes its on-track action uncomplicated and leaves nuances such as strategy and tire choice for specialist media to explain. One example of this stripped-back storytelling is its presentation of the battle between McLaren's Carlos Sainz and Renault's Daniel Ricciardo in S2:E3, "Dogfight." Ricciardo passes Sainz on track. Both pit at the same time. Sainz passes Ricciardo and goes on to finish four places ahead. Boom!

There's a little more to it than that. Ricciardo was faster in qualifying than Sainz and started behind him only because of a three-place grid penalty for an incident with Daniil Kvyat in Baku. When Ricciardo and Sainz pitted together, Sainz had medium-compound tires fitted while Ricciardo went with hard-compound Pirellis, which take longer to warm up. Hence the ease with which Sainz goes by. One shot in the montage shows Sainz on soft-compound tires later in the race, the kind of detail that enrages some F1 fans (tire compound can be identified by the color of the stripe on the tire wall).

The two drivers then ran closely until the safety car was deployed after Ricciardo's next pit stop. Sainz stopped while the safety car was on-track and his rivals were running slower, which gained him a position while Ricciardo lost one—and then got stuck behind his teammate.

Too much detail? You decide . . .

Around pit stop time you'll often hear a driver's engineer suggesting they will do the opposite of what the driver ahead does. If they pit, you stay out; if they stay out, you pit. The imperative for the leading driver to maintain track position gives the following driver a potential tactical advantage, especially at circuits whose configuration make the undercut effect powerful.

The most potent example of how the following driver can seize the moment came in the controversial finale to the 2021 race season at Abu Dhabi (*DTS* S4:E10). Lewis Hamilton was leading Max Verstappen when the safety car was deployed with a handful of laps remaining. Hamilton couldn't pit without giving up track position—if he did, Verstappen would stay out. So Verstappen pitted instead, fitting fresh tires—which gave him a decisive edge when the track went green.

Jargon Buster

Delta

Jargon Buster

Tire Offset

Perhaps one of F1's most infuriatingly pompous technical terms, "delta" simply refers to a time difference. It's generally used to describe the differences in potential lap times achievable by the three tire compounds available at each race, the difference between the lap times of two cars, or the gap between cars on track. During virtual safety car periods, drivers must stick to a set lap time (slower than racing speed) and the screens on their steering wheels will tell them whether they are "delta positive" or "delta negative," slower or faster, respectively, than the prescribed speed.

Tire offset is a difference in performance caused by a) the relative age of the tires in terms of laps completed or b) the types of tire compounds. Establishing tire offset is a popular way of gaining a strategic advantage. Teams do this at the start of the race by fitting a different compound than other cars, or they build it during the race by stopping at different times than immediate rivals either to achieve less wear or to fit an alternative tire compound.

 AROUND PIT STOP TIME YOU'LL OFTEN HEAR A DRIVER'S ENGINEER SUGGESTING THEY WILL DO THE OPPOSITE OF WHAT THE DRIVER AHEAD DOES."

Index

Page numbers in italics indicate an item in a photograph or caption.

Image Credits

Alamy Stock Photos: 2, dpa/Alamy Live News; 6, Florent Gooden/DPPI; 2, dpa/Alamy Live News; 9t, David Davies; 10, dpa/Alamy Live News; 12, dpa/Alamy Live News; 13, XPB Images Ltd/Alamy Live News; 14, XPB Images Ltd/Alamy Live News; 15r, Abaca Press; 16t, Antonin Vincent/DPPI; 16b, XPB Images Ltd/Alamy Live News; 17, DPPI; 18, DPPI; 19, XPB Images Ltd/Alamy Live News; 20, XPB Images Ltd/Alamy Live News; 21, XPB/Press Association Images; 22, James Moy; 23t, Florent Gooden/DPPI/LiveMedia; 23b, dpa/Alamy Live News; 24, Reuters/Hamad I Mohammed; 28, XPB Images Ltd/Alamy Live News; 30, Octane; 57, Moviestore Collection; 70, corleve; 72, Remko De Waal/ANP; 74, National Motor Museum/Heritage Images; 75, The Picture Art Collection; 76, Shawshots; 77t, Historic Collection; 77b, World History Archive; 78, Avpics; 79t, GPL-Fred Taylor; 79b, John Gaffen; 80t, XPB Images Ltd/Alamy Live News; 80b, height advantage; 81, Loop Images Ltd; 82, Florent Gooden/DPPI/LiveMedia; 83t, Claire Mackintosh; 84, XPB Images Ltd/Alamy Live News; 86, Avpics; 87, Antonin Vincent/DPPI/LiveMedia; 88, CJM Photography; 89, KS_Autosport; 90, XPB Images Ltd/Alamy Live News; 91, James Moy; 92, DPPI; 95t, IPA; 96, IPA; 98, GPL-Geoff Goddard; 99, Peter Seyfferth; 100, James Moy; 102, James Moy; 103, Geza Kurka; 104, speedpix; 105, Actionplus; 106, James Moy; 108t, s&g; 108b, Gergo Toth; 109t, dpa/Alamy Live News; 109b, David Davies; 110, David Kashakhi; 112, Nippon News; 113, DPPI; 114, Wenn Rights Ltd; 115, Juha Jarvinen; 116, Evgeny Glyanenko; 118, David Davies; 120, A.P.S. (UK); 122, James Moy; 124, Reuters/Hamad I Mohammed; 126, XPB Images Ltd/Alamy Live News; 128t, MiRafoto.com; 128bl, Photo12/Ann Ronan Picture Library; 128br, LiveMedia; 129t, Martyn Goddard; 129b, GPL-Franco Lini; 130, James Moy; 132, GPL-Geoff Goddard; 133t, National Motor Museum; 133b, CJM Photography; 134, corleve; 135, DPPI; 136, Leks Agency; 138, Tim Goode; 140, Xinhua; 141, DPPI; 142, dpa/Alamy Live News; 144, IPA; 145, Aly Song; 146, dan74; 147, dpa/Alamy Live News; 148, XPB Images Ltd/Alamy Live News; 150, Henadzi Pechan; 151, IPA; 153, corleve; 154, dpa/Alamy Live News; 156, Crispin Thruston; 159, dpa/Alamy Live News; 160, GPL-Bryn Williams; 161, Theodore Liasi;162, Oleg Konin; 164, Nippon News; 165, Marco A. Rezende/BrazilPhotos; 167, Avpics; 168, XPB Images Ltd/Alamy Live News; 170, Rula Rouhana; 171, Vipula Samarakoon; 172, Edgar Su; 173, LiveMedia; 174, James Lindley; 175, Mikalai Zastsenski; 177, Frank Nowikowski; 178, David Davies; 179, Steve Etherington; 180t, Octane; 180b, DPPI; 181, James Moy; 182, James Moy; 184, Bender Rodriguez; 190, Action Plus Sports Images.

LAT Images: 4, Mark Sutton; 9b, Glenn Dunbar; 26, Steve Etherington; 27, Sutton Images; 31, Charles Coates; 32, Carl Bingham; 34, 35, Steve Etherington; 36, Rainer Schlegelmilch; 37; 38; 39, David Phipps; 40; 41, Rainer Schlegelmilch; 42, David Phipps; 44; 45; 46, David Phipps; 48; 49, David Phipps; 50, David Phipps; 51, David Phipps; 52; 54; 56, Sutton Images; 58, Rainer Schlegelmilch; 60; 61, Andy Hone; 62, Sutton Images; 63; 64, Sutton Images; 66, Patrik Lundin; 68, Daniel Kalisz; 69, Sutton Images; 94, Rainer Schlegelmilch; 95b, Giorgio Piola; 105, Peter Nygard; 147, Sutton Images; 174, Jerry Andre.

Acknowledgments

Thanks to everyone who has helped bring this book to fruition: the tag team of my editor, Dennis Pernu, and project manager, Brooke Pelletier, for their enthusiasm and patience (the latter sorely tested); and Box To Box films, whose endlessly entertaining show has opened the eyes of a whole new audience to Formula 1… though this audience still doesn't include my wife, Julie, who I'd like to thank specially for her continued love and support, or my cats, who continue to prefer to sleep on Sunday afternoons. They will remain in the dark about the fact that any of my on-camera appearances in Drive to Survive ended up on the cutting room floor…

First Published in 2023 by Motorbooks, an imprint of The Quarto Group,

100 Cummings Center, Suite 265-D, Beverly, MA 01915, USA.
T (978) 282-9590 F (978) 283-2742 Quarto.com

Motorbooks titles are also available at discount for retail, wholesale, promotional, and bulk purchase. For details, contact the Special Sales Manager by email at specialsales@quarto.com or by mail at The Quarto Group, Attn: Special Sales Manager, 100 Cummings Center, Suite 265-D, Beverly, MA 01915, USA.

26 25 24 23 22   1 2 3 4 5

ISBN: 978-0-7603-8067-3

Digital edition published in 2023

eISBN: 978-0-7603-8069-7

Library of Congress Cataloging-in-Publication Data
Names: Codling, Stuart, 1972- author.
Title: Formula 1 drive to survive, unofficial companion : the stars, strategy, technology, and history of F1 / Stuart Codling.
Other titles: Formula one drive to survive, unofficial companion
Description: Beverly, MA : Motorbooks, 2023. | Includes index. | Summary:
"The Formula 1 Drive to Survive Unofficial Companion takes new and longtime F1 fans beyond the personalities and drama to contextualize technology, rules, strategy, and history"-- Provided by publisher.
Identifiers: LCCN 2022047402 | ISBN 9780760380673 | ISBN 9780760380697 (ebook)
Subjects: LCSH: Grand Prix racing--History. | FIA Formula One World Championship--History. | Formula One automobiles--History.
Classification: LCC GV1029.15 .C639 2023 | DDC 796.7209--dc23/eng/20221116
LC record available at https://lccn.loc.gov/2022047402

Design: www.traffic-design.co.uk
Page Layout: www.traffic-design.co.uk

Printed in China

Cover Images: Main: Dominique Mollee/Alamy Stock Photo; Background: SOPA Images/Alamy Stock Photo
Back cover: James Moy/Alamy Live News Stock Photo